To God be all the honor and all the glory forever and ever Amen

This book is dedicated to the work of God and to all of His saints who work tirelessly in the endeavor to bring His kingdom to the lost and possibly the last generation the Church of Jesus Christ will reach. It is my sincere wish that the reader, begin with prayer before reading this book. We pray that the Holy Spirit guide your mind and heart in understanding how to apply its contents. For each of us is accountable to God in reaching all the souls He has prepared for his church.

ACKNOWLEDGMENTS

This book is truly a result of countless years in the making. It has taken a span of years to witness the needs of attracting visitors in Hispanic churches. As a result of this need, I was lead to the endeavor of learning how visitors are attracted to churches through higher education and field experience. This project is an attempt to put into words and concepts the ideas and solutions to problems I have found.

This work would never have materialized in its form had it not been impacted, inspired and supported by so many people that only the rosters in heaven will be able to mention them all. I desire to thank those who without their help, this work would only have been a dream.

I am especially grateful to my wife, Linda, who has encouraged me always in my work. She saw the need of God's people to be better equipped. She proven her tireless dedication to see this work be published. She has been my source of inspiration in many times of weakness.

I desire to thank my twelve-year-old son, Nathanael Lawrence, who is my joy and my second best friend. He too, has sacrificed his time with his father so that I could finish this work. Their support is the reason why we today

Published by Lor-Lin Ministries
A Division of A. I. M. Seminars
Harlingen, Texas 78550
Printed in U.S.A.,

Scripture quotations used in this book are from
HOLY BIBLE, The Open Bible edition.
© 1975, by Thomas Nelson Inc.,
Used by permission Thomas Nelson Publishers
Nashville, Tennessee.

© Copyright 1998 by Lorenzo V. Gonzalez

Library of Congress C. N. # 98-092269

All rights reserved.

ISBN-13:978-1-892874-00-9

ISBN-10:1-892874-00-8

This book was formerly written as a
Doctoral thesis for Talbot School of
Theology-Biola University

Subtitle

CHURCH VISITORS:
METHODS OF ATTRACTION AND
RETENTION FOR HISPANIC CHURCHES

Cover Design by Jose Lopez
Edited in English by Laura Mcintosh

Attracting Visitors to Hispanic Churches

Dr. Lorenzo V. Gonzalez

AIM SEMINARS

Write to

lorenzogonz@sbcglobal.net

have this aid to offer to all the pastors, ministers and lay people. Special thanks to Benjamin Lopez, who in a limited amount of time translated and did the page layout of the Spanish version of this book.

I would also like to extend my gratitude and thanks to the Apostolic Assembly, in the Faith of Christ Jesus, Inc. for their support and trust in permitting me to use some of their material in this project.

In addition, I would like to thank Pastor and Secretary of Christian Education of the Apostolic Assembly, Samuel Valverde for his help and support.

I also would like to express my sincere thanks to all the Pastors who have extended their churches and congregations to try and test various methods of visitor Attraction and programs of church growth.

The Art work for both the English and Spanish book covers were created by our very own artist in the Christian Education art Department. The artist is a young man who I had the pleasure of working with, Jose Lopez.

There are countless of people that contributed suggestion throughout the course of this book and to all of them am very grateful and pray that they will continue to encourage one another in the name of our lord Jesus Christ.

V.

TABLE OF CONTENTS

LIST OF FIGURES ·········· vi
LIST OF TABLES ··········· viii
INTRODUCTION TO THE PROJECT ······· 1
    The Need for This Study ············ 3
    The Rationale for the Project ········ 12
    The Basic Assumptions ············ 13
    The Intended Outcome ············ 14
    Definitions ····················· 15
    Biblical and Theological Issues ········ 18
    Literature Review ················ 25
    Design of the Study ·············· 37
    The Procedures and Evaluation of the
    Manuscript ···················· 39
    Summary ····················· 40

CHAPTER
    1. Introduction ·················· 43
    Concept of Visitor Attraction and Retention ··· 45
    Summary ····················· 54
    2. Heritage ···················· 56
    History of the Hispanic Church Development ··56
    Current State of the Hispanic ········· 61

    Contour of the Hispanic People · · · · · · · · · · ·82

    Action Steps ·85

    Summary · 86

3. Strengths and Weaknesses

    Evaluating the Local Church and Its Leaders · 88

    Resources for Evaluations · · · · · · · · · · · · · · ·91

    Reasons for Evaluating Workers · · · · · · · · · · 93

    Defining Low Morale · · · · · · · · · · · · · · · · · · 99

    Spiritual Gifts ·100

    Godly Vision and Direction · · · · · · · · · · · · · 109

    Godly Leadership · 110

    Action Steps · 116

    Summary · 117

4. Community Evaluation

    Assessing Community Needs · · · · · · · · · · · · 121

    Culture Changing Communities · · · · · · · · · · 121

    Size of the Community · · · · · · · · · · · · · · · · 127

    Boundaries in the Community · · · · · · · · · · · ·133

    Assessing Cultural Demands · · · · · · · · · · · · 139

    Demand for Choices and Variety · · · · · · · · · 143

    Action Steps · 145

    Summary · 146

5. Generational Contours and Their Effects

- Generational Ideology · 150
- Generations of Today · 160
- Living Generations in America · · · · · · · · · · · · · 152
- Generational Descriptions · · · · · · · · · · · · · · · · · 157
- G. I. Descriptions · 158
- Silent Generation · 159
- Baby Boom Generation · · · · · · · · · · · · · · · · · · · 162
- Baby Buster Generation · · · · · · · · · · · · · · · · · · · 168
- Boomlets or Millennial Children · · · · · · · · · · · · · 170
- Hispanic Generation Values · · · · · · · · · · · · · · · 172
- Hispanic Generations · 182
- The Traditionalist · 183
- The Inbetweener · 185
- The Challenger · 187
- The Synthesizer · 189
- Action Steps · 191
- Summary · 191

6. Visitor Attraction and Retention

- Profile of a Nation and a Church · · · · · · · · · · · 192
- Levels of Trust · 196

Recognition of Trust Transfer · · · · · · · · · · · · · 197

Bonding with Other Cultures · · · · · · · · · · · · · · · ·198

Contours of the Congregation · · · · · · · · · · · · · · 196

The Church and Technology · · · · · · · · · · · · · · ·205

People's Pathways and Flow · · · · · · · · · · · · · · · 206

Summary ·213

7. Conclusion to the Book

Linking the Unchurched to the Congregation 216

What Well Ministries Have in Common · · · · ·218

Biblical Well Meetings · · · · · · · · · · · · · · · · · · · 219

Evaluation to the Book · · · · · · · · · · · · · · · · · · 234

The Inception of the Project · · · · · · · · · · · · · · · 234

Research and Development · · · · · · · · · · · · · · · 235

The Readers · 241

Evaluations and Conclusions· · · · · · · · · · · · · 243

Questions for Further Study · · · · · · · · · · · · · · 243

Implications for Church at Large · · · · · · · · · · 244

Summary · 245

BIBLIOGRAPHY · 231

LIST OF FIGURES

<u>Figure</u>   <u>Page</u>

1. Sociological cycle model 4
2. Mobergs model 7
3. Sociological cycle model 61
4. Partial Sociological cycle view of the church in Antioch 65
5. Early Structure of power displayed at the organizational stage 68
6. Later structure or power shift In the organizational stage 69
7. David Moberg's model 71
8. The Joshua model 78
9. The King's model 80
10. The Deliverance Generational Cycle 155
11. The King's generational cycle 155
12. Forces 173
13. Four value systems 174
14. Hispanic generations 182
15. The Traditionalists 183

FIGURE

PAGE

16. The Inbetweener · 185

17. The Challenger · 187

18. The Synthesizer · 189

LIST OF TABLES

Table	Page
The Generational cycle in America · · · · · · · · · · · · · · ·	152
Living Generations in America · · · · · · · · · · · · · · · · · ·	153
Generations from the Great Power and Millennial cycles ·	161

INTRODUCTION TO THE PROJECT

In a culture where church membership is not assigned or required, the problem of how to attract visitors becomes critical. In the Hispanic culture, as in others, the people who seek a church on their own are usually on the last road to finding a solution or an answer for their pain or suffering. These people are hurting so much that they are seeking a solution to their dilemma. The number of people seeking a church is usually too small in comparison with the numbers a church needs to keep growing. Thus, the problem of finding and attracting visitors for any church is very important for the long term health of a congregation.

Kirk C. Hadaway writes:
> A church must be able to attract a steady stream of visitors because only a small percentage of those who visit will eventually join; and because this is a very mobile society, a regular supply If additions is necessary in order for churches just to stay even and avoid decline-much less to start growing. [1]

A church grows by three means. The first is called biological growth, i.e., via the birth of babies into the fold of the church. The second method is called transfer growth. This is the growth that usually happens when

---

1 Kirk C. Hadaway, Church Growth) Principles; Separating fact from fiction: (Nashville, TN: Broadman Press, 1991), 125.

people move from church to church. The third method is called new convert growth. This is the method of bring new members into a church through evangelism

Other than through biological growth, it is important that a church learns how to attract new visitors. What may attract one person or a family may not necessarily attract another person or family. What may attract people from one culture may not necessarily attract those from another culture. Herein lies the dilemma of developing a workable plan of attracting and retaining visitors. Too often in the past churches have targeted one culture or one type of people to ensure church growth.

Today, new communities with mixed cultures and peoples are developing faster than at any other time in history. Even planned communities are catering to selected people in regard to age, status of life, or wealth. Older and more established residential areas are undergoing cultural changes as younger people move away from home and their parents retire to other areas.

There is no guarantee for an established, long-resident church in a community to find the culture or even the kind of people it desires to attract in sufficient numbers to allow the church to continue growing.

THE NEED FOR THIS STUDY

The proposed book manuscript is intended to answer the question: How can small Hispanic churches attract and retain visitors? In the 1950s, Hispanic Pentecostal churches were on the upswing numerically. They were primarily fast-paced churches with dynamic music and popular, people-oriented styles of worship. The churches were evangelistically aggressive. However, in the last few decades, the Pentecostal churches have passed through what has been called "The Sociological Cycle," and will no doubt pass through all the levels through which other denominations have gone. The Sociological Cycle consists of four stages that denominations grow through in time. Originally, the Pentecostal movement was viewed as a sect, but recently has moved toward the third stage, denomination.

The Pentecostal movement in the United States, along with other post Pentecostal movements such as the Apostolic Assemblies, United Apostolic or Pentecostal denominations, which are strictly Jesus Name movements, are today experiencing the second and in some cases the third stage of the Sociological Cycle. They are not the only ones who have had a problem in moving through these

areas; most Trinitarian movements that have organized into some structure of an assembly or denomination have experienced the same problems. Some of these movements have become entrenched in the second or institutional stage or level, while others have gone on through the entire Sociological Cycle. The following diagram is taken Town's book,
America's Fastest Growing Churches. 2

Fig. 1. The above diagram is taken from Towns' book, America's Fastest growing Churches and will be compared to Troeltsch's , model in chapter two.

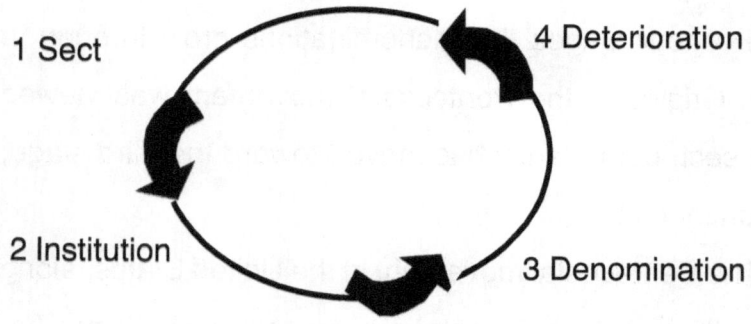

1 Sect

4 Deterioration

2 Institution

3 Denomination

---

2 Elmer L. Towns, America's Fastest Growing Churches (Nashville, TN: Impact Books, 1972), 156.

In the late 1920's, a German philosopher-sociologist by the name of Ernst Troeltch wrote about the churches that grow from a sect status to ecclesia/assembly, or what today would be termed the denominational stage. Troeltch's model begins as a sect and then moves to become an institution. It then moves to the stage of a fully organized denomination, and finally will end at the deterioration stage.

Many students and authors that have studied this cycle of growth have given Troeltch's model other names. For example, the first or sect stage has been termed the fundamentalism stage. The second stage of this cycle has been labeled institution. The third stage is known as denomination, and the final cycle is theological liberalism. Some even combine denomination and theological liberalism together in the same stage.

Today the institutional stage is called by many the organizational stage. The need of the organizational stage is what builds the infrastructure of a church, organization, or denomination and allows the infrastructure to develop the government rules, guidelines, constitution, and officers. This in turn forces the denomination stage to begin to process itself. The dynamic tension between the organization and the denomination stages causes the inversion of power, freedom, strength, and resources of local churches to the top of the organization. Leaders at this level have discovered that in order to manage the institution stage effectively, all the power must be at the helm. A total and complete transfer of power from local churches to a headquarters means that local churches will be told what and how much they can do at the local level of the church.

There appear to be two points of critical importance in the development of this cycle. The first is between the sect and institution stages, and the second is between the institution and the denomination stages. In order to develop understanding of what is happening to the Hispanic churches, David Moberg's model needs to be investigated.

David's Moberg, a church sociologist from Marquette University, has developed a cycle of his own that should be examined. He sees a *"process by which cults originate, develop into sects, and then into denominations, perhaps finally to emerge from the process as churches."*[3]

---

[3] David O. Moberg, The Church or a Social Institution (Englewood Clifts, NJ: Prentice-Hall, Inc., 1962), 100.

David Moberg's model can help explain the two points of critical importance n the development cycle. Most cult-like churches that have undergone Moberg's cycle can attest to the first stage of cult to sect. Depending on the psychological and theological standing and philosophy of ministry of the initial cult leaders, the tension of growth from cult to sect can be a critical one. All along the time line of church history, there have been cult leaders that their psychological and theological standing and philosophy of ministry did not permit it them to grow into a sect. The tension of growth from cult to sect can be a critical one because the cult leaders see the growth as a present danger to themselves and their cult members. Their belief in themselves and their mission hinder the process.

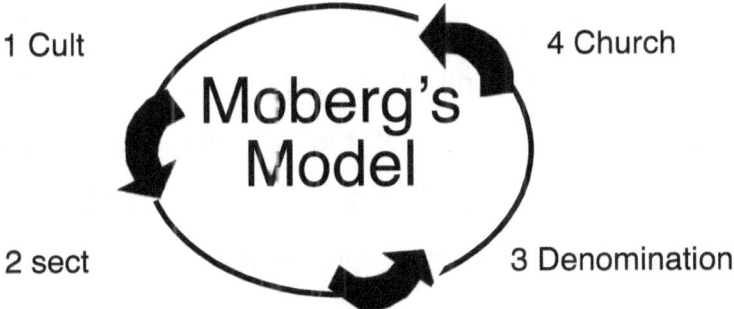

Fig. 2. The above diagram is taken from Towns' book, America's Fastest growing Churches and will be compared to Troeltsch's , model in chapter 2.

Some cults, where the leadership comes from one man, can have selfish reasons why the leader does not desire the cult to continue and will even guide it away from the process of development.

The second point of critical importance in the development of Moberg's cycle is between sect and denomination. The critical point develops when the infrastructure needed begins to form in the organization phase. In the organization phase or cycle the guidelines, rules, officers are devised and written into some sort of a constitution.. This is Constitution then becomes binding to the point, in some cases, having more power than the Word of God. Depending on the men that develop this constitution and their ability to foresee the needs off future generations, the constitution can become the organization's future worst enemy. This critical point does not seem at first to make any difference, but it is not until three or more generations have functioned under the constitutional tutorage, and all the amendments added by others, that it becomes the noose that slowly chokes the church. When the leader/s of a cult do not allow their cult to process into a church, they usually end up in a similar situation like that of the Davidian Branch in Waco, Texas.

According to Elmer Towns, it is the denomination stage that reduces or enhances growth in the local church. Depending on the makeup of the constitution, either it helps the local churches or it helps the organizational infrastructure. Towns puts it into this perspective: *"Liberalism or mainline denominationalism does not have the religious dynamic to naturally attract individuals. When the attendance at denominational-type churches climbs, it does so for extraneous reasons of an external pressure for growth or their spiritual life is void, hence they have no internal dynamic for growth."*[4]

Elmer Towns is saying in the quote above that the denomination will expect the local church to grow naturally, but will probably not help it grow. Churches in a denomination will grow in attendance only if they do not play by the rules set forth by that denomination. The reason is that the denomination usually feeds off of the local churches instead of feeding them. The local church usually develops its style of organization from either the denomination standards or from the constitution, but not from the experience of the pastor and leaders who understand the needs of their congregation or community of lost souls.

---

4 Towns, 157.

Usually, the style of organization is from earlier decades of church polity.

Today, churches need to rethink their philosophy of ministry to see if it is leading the church towards a healthy growth. It must, by its sheer need to evangelize and reach the lost, construct popular programs and activities to bring salvation to those whom tile Holy Spirit desires to save.

However, it is the local church, with its limited resources, that feeds the infrastructure of the denominational organization with much needed leaders, money, and programs. By using. Its limited resources and manpower for the denominational needs, the local church restricts and debilitates its own evangelical work. When the local church uses most of its resources in this capacity, it ceases to work to its fullest potential in reaching the lost. The attendance of visitors drops drastically, and so does the growth of the local church. Add to the burden of having limited resources and manpower the demand for the denomination for the pastors and churches to support programs, services, and other types of activities outside the local church, which squander the limited time for the churches to have revivals and increase their visitor attraction and retention.

The result is the crippling effect that denominations causes to the local churches. What started once as a greatly needed programs, services and activities can later become the barriers of church growth.

It is a well-known fact that larger denominations do not place total emphasis on reaching the lost because they feel that this is the responsibility of the local church. Their responsibility is to create the infrastructure that allows communication and direction between the local churches and headquarters. Because denominations consider themselves the head of the organization, they can lose perspective and consume the limited resources of the body for their own purposes. When this occurs, the local church is drained of most of its resources. This is the danger that many organized church assemblies are currently facing.

A balance must be struck by the local churches and the denomination. This balance must favor the local church and not the denomination. The denomination must always remember that its purpose is a global one, whereas the local church is there for the local community. The denomination must at all times streamline itself and keep focused on he work it has been called to do.

The denomination must stay in focused with such challenges as the global missionary outreach and the planting of local churches in areas that have not yet been established. The balance between the needs of the denomination and the local church must constantly be evaluated.

In summary, this study is needed to aid pastors in acquiring ideas and methods for reaching the lost with the limited resources available to the local church. This will be done by showing leaders how to maximize visitor attraction and retention.

THE RATIONALE FOR THE PROJECT

This project is to be a book manuscript written in popular style. It is meant to aid leaders, pastors, and anyone working in area of evangelism. This manuscript is written to provide Hispanic churches with an understanding of what hinders today's small church in attracting and retaining visitors and of how to find workable strategies for church growth. An increase in understanding and overcoming expansion barriers today along with strategic, well-devised programs and activities can produce a substantial visitor flow, which will allow all churches to grow much more quickly. Because of the number of people and finances available to the local churches, their options are limited, and most must make maximum use of their time and resources if they are to grow. The writer of this dissertation has been involved in church growth in the past seven years with the Apostolic Assembly of the Faith in Christ Jesus, which is a corporation of approximately 600 predominantly Spanish-speaking churches. During this time, this writer has been able to personally visit and/or study about half the churches. Field research has shown the need of many churches to develop new approaches to ministry in the new millennia. This project will help provide insight for these churches.

THE BASIC ASSUMPTIONS

The underlying aim of this dissertation action project is to introduce pastors, leaders and local church evangelists to strategies for reaching unchurched people. Many churches are being pastored in the same style devised through the middle part of this century. The same programs and activities are being used today as in the 50's. The 90's decade has a different kind of audience than that of the 30's through 50's. Thus, the church needs updated programs and ways to attract and retain visitors. The following assumptions are important to the development of this project:

1. It is assumed that most small church pastors are still using methods that worked well in the church before the 60's.

2. It is assumed that some pastors discovered new methods which are more effective in the 90's.

3. It is assumed that if all churches used these newer methods, church attendance would increase significantly by members and visitors.

THE INTENDED OUTCOME

It is intended that this dissertation project will result in a book manuscript that will eventually be published in Spanish for the use of Hispanic leaders. This dissertation is designed to accomplish future goals:

1. It is intended to help local church leaders understand their function of reaching the lost by better understanding the needs of visitors.

2. It is intended to be a tool to assist churches in developing a ministry of visitor attraction by educating its members in this important ministry.

3. It is intended to be a guide for denominations in the fine art of balancing resources, time and personnel between local church denominational expansion.

4. It is also intended to help the local church in retaining 100% of the visitors it currently attracts.

DEFINITIONS

Several definitions are central to this project:

1. <u>Church visitors</u> refer to those people visiting a church for the first or consecutive time who are not members in any church.

2. <u>Attraction</u> is a process that represents the church and its members to visitors to persuade them to come to hear the Gospel of salvation in a church.

3. <u>Retention</u> is a process whereby a church is able to retain these visitors and incorporate them into the fold of a church.

4. <u>Hispanic Church</u> is that part of the body of Christ composed of Hispanics (Mexicans, Puerto Ricans, Haitians, Cubans, Central and South American Natives, etc., as well as North American Hispanic Natives).

5. <u>Hispanic pastor</u> is usually the shepherd of any of the previously mentioned Hispanic churches.

6. <u>Poor results</u> are the outcome of long time endeavors with little or no numerical gain.

7. <u>Attracting results</u> are the outcome of endeavors with a substantial numerical gain or increase.

8. <u>Increasing results</u> are the outcome of continual Implementation of new ideas and strategy.

9. <u>Methods</u> refer to a procedure or process for attaining an object.

10. <u>Programs</u> are the activities used to pursue or embrace desired outcomes.

11. <u>Activities</u> are vigorous or energetic actions to acquire given functions.

12. <u>Strategy</u> is the use of careful planning or making preparations towards a goal.

13. <u>Culture</u> is the sum total of socially learned ways of living: values, customs, beliefs, aesthetic values, linguistic expression, patterns of thinking and perceiving norms, and styles of communication which a group of people has developed to assure its functional operation and survival in a particular physical and environment context.

14. <u>Sup-culture</u> is a group of people within a sociopolitical structure who share cultural characteristics (often linguistic) which are distinctive enough to distinguish it from others within the same society.

15. <u>Race</u> is a somewhat suspect concept used (but often misused) to identify large groups of humans who share a more or less distinctive combination of genetic and hereditary physical characteristics.

16. <u>Class</u> is a stratum of people within a society who share basic economic, political, educational, or cultural characteristics that give them advantage or disadvantage in the societal system.

17. <u>Cross-cultural Communication</u> is the transmission of messages from a sender to a receiver from different cultural backgrounds in one or more of a variety of codes - both verbal and nonverbal, including language, gestures, signs, written and non-written symbols, etc., to which the sender and the receiver attach meaning. The aim of communication is to transfer the message with as little loss of meaning as possible.

18. <u>Contextualization</u> is fitting the focus of context, theological approach, and communication technique of the Gospel to context' of a particular people and culture.

BIBLICAL AND THEOLOGICAL ISSUES

Very little is found in the Bible concerning visitor attraction and retention because the early church was not fully established. The biblical material presented will be studied to determine its effect on the issue of identifying ways that Scripture deals with situations of attracting and retaining visitors.

The story of the woman at Jacob's well found in John 4 is a key Scripture passage which illustrates an important method of approaching possible converts.[5] It seems that the Lord Jesus went out of His way to be at the well at the sixth hour when it is customary for women to draw water. Jesus opened a conversation with the Samaritan woman at the well on the topic of water. Jesus could have drawn His own water from the well. In fact, this is probably what any other Jewish rabbi would have done.

This seemed to be the disciples' same thought when they found their rabbi speaking to the Samaritan woman at the well in verse 27.

---

[5] The Gospel of John 4: 1-42, the conversation with the woman at the well.

The conversation between the woman and Jesus is a unique one. Jesus presented Himself to this woman as the living water (verse 10). He proved to her who He was by revealing her current life of sin. Seeing that He was no ordinary man, she asked Him if He was a prophet or the Christ (verses 19 and 25). The whole conversation led to her finding Christ and then going to town to bring others to Christ.

This passage teaches that the church is to go wherever souls are, regardless of who they are, and attract them by some means to the Gospel of Jesus Christ. This is exactly what Jesus does by first obeying His father's word in going to the lost sheep of Israel. Verse four states that He, by necessity, had to cross through Samaria. This necessity teaches the lesson of taking the Gospel to a people or group no one else will approach. Christ attracted the Samaritan woman by asking her for water, and this allowed 'the prejudice between the Jews and the Samaritans to surface. He then addressed the spiritual need of the woman by confronting her with her with her current marital situation. Through this encounter, Christ developed a model to use in attracting visitors.

Another key passage can be found in the book of Acts Where the apostle Paul discussed Christ and His resurrection with a group of Jews and Greeks.

The place is known as Mars Hill where the structure of the Areopagus stood and the council of the areopagus met to hear strangers speak of new teachings. It was here that the apostle Paul was invited to speak of this new teaching. The apostle Paul began by speaking about God and His plan to send His Son to die for the people's sins. He used an altar that Athenians placed in memory of the UNKNOWN GOD. This altar was built by the Athenians to appease any god that might have been offended because there was no idol or statue in his name. The apostle Paul used this altar to the UNKNOWN God to introduce his God and Christ.

The church, too, can look for such things to open up conversations with people who are not converts. The Mars Hill incident was done on purpose by the apostle Paul to establish a common ground of conversation. This method that the Apostle Paul used is similar to the one Jesus used with the Samaritan woman. Church members, too, can look for similar opportunities to established common grounds of interest and invite people to church.

In the book <u>Always Advancing</u>, Daniel Reeves has a chapter entitleded "Prescriptions and Pathways" in which he writes:

"Several new measures that are helping con

gregations to plan programs more effectively relate to growth pathways . . . . Another term for growth pathways is people flow; that is, the means by which unchurched families move toward responsible membership. This flow involves the conversion, restoration, and maturation processes . . . people flow systems provide the framework for goal setting, for strategy preparation, and for measuring effectiveness. People flow analysts are sensitive to persons in change. They believe that many of the present strategies are ineffective because church growth workers are working against the flow of social movements. Upward mobility is a reality of present society. As a neutral force, it can work for or against church growth. Churches that recognize its values can provide the appropriate recognition of persons caught in its current. ., Such adjustments illustrate the difference between upstream (against the flow strategists also recognize and anticipate social currents."[7]

Dr. Reeves further explains the Lord's mission at the well. Jacob's well presents a pathway where people of that day used to Come to acquire water for their daily use. Christ represents the Christian searching for these path-

---

[7] Daniel Reeves, <u>Always Advancing: Modern Strategies for Church Growth</u> (San Bernandino, CA: Here's Life Publishers, Inc., 1984), pgs. 67-70.

ways and used to Come to acquire water for their daily use. Christ represents the Christian searching for these pathways and the woman is the visitor who is searching for living water. The conversation between two is certainly evangelistic, and the result is Christ staying two additional days in that town. There was a possibly of repentance, since there was evidence of people's hearts changing. This incident reveals the fact that visitor attraction does not necessarily to happen in the entrance to a sanctuary. Visitor attraction can be any method with any person, program, activity or process in any place, by anyone. The same is true with visitor retention. This work does not necessarily have to be on the church grounds.

Another example of visitor attraction is found in Acts 11:11-26. This is the famous passage where the disciples of Christ are first called Christians. In this passage many believers went to various cities away from Jerusalem because of the incident of Stephen's death and their fear of persecution. Some of these disciples arrived in the city of Antioch. There they began to spread the good news of Christ and soon raised a small gathering of listeners or visitors. In order to retain and convert these visitors, the Jerusalem church sent Barnabas to Antioch. Upon arriving in the city of Antioch, Barnabas began to utilize his gift of organization and organized the fellowship.

Seeing that he needed preaching and teaching gifts, which apparently he did not have, he felt the need to invite Saul of Tarsus to come join him in the harvesting of those saints.

This type of evangelism is similar to the approach used before by Jesus in attracting visitors. The method for attracting visitors was the preaching of the Gospel. This Scripture clearly teaches that through the teaching, preaching and fellowshipping of the saints, visitors will be attracted to the church, possibly resulting in conversion. Today, many church leaders are turned off by the word "evangelism," especially as it pertains to the door-to-door process.

Joe Aldrich in his book <u>Life Style Evangelism</u> writes:

> "Because of exposure to unhealthy evangelism models, the evangelism enterprise has been hurt. Often it is the methodology of some of these models which offends the sensitivities of caring Christians. Sometimes they are artificial and unnatural. Many Christians have personal objections to some of the approaches to "wining" the lost. Gimmicks, pseudo-questionnaires, buttonholing, evangelical mugging, and the outright rudeness of some witnesses turn them off. The end result is that evangelism becomes a much misunderstood term; one which most people either swear by it ... or at."[8]

---

[8] Joe Aldrich, <u>Life Style Evangelism</u> (Portland, OR: Multnomah Press, 1981), pg. 19, ers, Inc., 1984), pgs. 67-70.

Many evangelistic workers have been ill-treated by the very same people to whom they are trying to witness. It takes very special people to continually keep up a good attitude of reaching people for Christ when people are constantly shutting doors in their faces and calling them names. Recent research in the northern part of the state of Texas discovered that of roughly fifty homes visited, one in six homes actually opened its doors to see who was knocking, and one in ten was actually willing to talk. Of those fifty homes, only two seemed to be interested in the Gospel. It is no wonder that many leaders feel that sending people out on cold-call evangelism is useless. Yet, the prospect of visitors in any church always seems to liven up any congregation.

New terminology along with new ideas, programs, activities and methods must be presented to churches in order to increase the size of the churches' work forces. Hispanic churches, traditionally Pentecostal, need new ways to energize their people and leaders to reach new people with the Gospel.

Today the local church, with the capacity to evangelize and witness, stands, with its buildings and denominational governments starved for workers. Reaching people with the Gospel in some churches is a lost art. If the local church is to inherit the kingdom of God, it needs to turn all of its remaining resources and personnel towards the goal of becoming full Gospel, total evangelistic, and culturally sensitive to the needs of the unchurched.

LITERATURE REVIEW

The need for a book on a topic such as visitor attraction and retention for Hispanic churches has been over due. Hispanic churches have for the last few decades been struggling to attract and retain visitors. In fact, young pastors today believe that yesterday's methodology and programs are clearly outdated and new ones must be invented and worked out in order to increase visitor attendance in local churches. Small local churches are not desiring perchance to grow their congregational size into the thousands, but on the other hand, they want to continue growing. Because there are crowds of unchurched people separated by generational differences, separate and distinct styles of worship preaching must be held at various times during the week to reach America's lost. Because this phenomenon has caught many small churches by surprise, pastors and church leaders are seeking new ways of translating the needs of these generations of lost souls into church liturgical philosophies of ministry.

One of the few books in this field has been written by Robert L. Blast. In his book <u>Attracting New Members</u>, he gives an overview of the procedures in developing a great plan in all visitors. He is the minister of evangelism for the Reformed Church in America, affording him much understanding in the field of attracting visitors. Though what he states may be advantageous for most English speaking churches and has much to offer, I believe it lacks understanding of what other cultures need. It is obvious that he did not intend to Write for a global setting. On the other hand, sometimes certain things said are principles that can translate into other cultures. This is what is important in his and other books: whether what he and others state can directly translate into other cultures, or whether it is unique to the specific culture directed by the author. Blast's book overall is beneficial for a general guide line to follow. He writes and outlines his chapters well and draws the reader to understand the process of attracting to incorporating the visitor into church membership. An evident weakness is that he gives very few examples citing churches and pastors doing such work. This generally is a draw back of the writer not having sufficient direct experience in the field he is writing about.

One example is in chapter 3 where Blast gives three steps for attracting the first-time visitor. Step #1 is advertising, step #2 is programing and step #3 is inviting. He quotes Lyle Schaller that a church should spend a minimum of 5% of its budget on advertising. He goes on to state that what ought to be advertised is the program of the church. In his third step he points out that the best method of attracting s getting the church to invite. Any restaurant owner or merchant will claim that they all advertise. They will state that it does pay to advertise, but their 95+ % of people that come and buy from businesses come because of word of mouth advertisement. Blast only spent one page in this most important third step.

In the opinion of many other authors, step three is the first one that should be applied. Because inviting is the most successful and the only resource on which the church can rely, it should be explored to its fullest extent. It is the take-off step into other points. Only after successfully committing the Church to spending time, money, and personnel in the most important agent bringing in visitors should the church then consider to use methods that are considerably less useful to the church.

Another earlier work on attracting and retaining visitors and church members is a book entitled How to Attract

And Keep Active Church Members by Donald P. Smith. The bulk of the material in this book deals with growing the church through membership retention. Coming from a Presbyterian background where the mainstream Protestant was in a steep membership decline, he poses some interesting facts and ideas on how to slow down the decline and maybe even stop it completely. The book often uses Presbyterian terminology. However, the findings apply to other denominations.

Though the book, strictly speaking, works with the attractions and retention suggestions for membership, some of the ideas can help the attraction of visitors. For example, in chapter two, Smith is talking about meeting different needs of church members as a way of bonding the various church members to each other. These very same ideas can work between members and visitors. He notes that, "bonding church es meet the different needs of their members. Some do it naturally, and others purposefully."[9]

He believes that a church ought to meet people's spiritual, social, psychological and physical needs, or it will not grow. However, not just the members need this healing, so do the unchurched that visit the church.

---

9 Donald P. Smith, How to Attract and Keep Active Church Members (Louisville, KY: West minster/John Knox Press, 1992), pg. 23.

Another interesting and cross-dimensional principle is the chapter on friendship ties and activities. Smith goes on to prove in chapter three that caring love and meaning for living are like the resin and hardener in epoxy glue. "Together they cement a member's loyalty to the congregation. If either is diminished, bonding suffers."[10]

Smith cites the reasons why churches have forgotten to be friendly. He states:

> "The pressures of our mobile society have fragmented life for most Americans. Therefore, it is especially important for the church to enable development of significant friendship. Our culture has shifted from local community to extended family, to nuclear family and finally to the lonely individual moving from place to place, and institution to institution, dealing with each if, and as, it serves his needs and interests."[11]

He believes that the fragmentation that this society has undergone has created a vacuum in the area of developing friendship. People in congregations must relearn how to develop and mature friendship relationships.

In the book, <u>Church Growth Principles: Separating Fact from Fiction,</u> by Kirk C. Hadaway, there is much information regarding Visitation. He points out in his first

---

10 Smith., Pg. 35.

11 Smith., Pg. 47.

Chapter that a church that is growing has at its banner intentional growth. He cites several authors as saying, "visitation is emphasized in Sunday school growth campaigns, in witness training programs, and in most books on church growth."[12] He proceeds to cite Callahan, Larry Lewis, Lyle Schaller, and Paul Powell as men who have written books on visitation and attracting visitors.

Hadaway points also to using revivals and special events to reach visitors. He asks: "Are revivals, high attendance days, and other special events related to church growth?" His answer is "yes, if used properly."[13] He cites surveys as showing that as much as 90% of growing churches have high attendance of visitors days. He goes on to prove that churches with plateaued or declining membership have as much as one-third to one-half of the number of visitors attracted by techniques of outreach.

Hadaway states: "Revivals, Friendship days, High Attendance Sundays, Giant Visitor Days, Pack a Pew Sundays, Super Sundays, and so forth can result in growth, but Apparently,

---

12 C. Kirk Hadaway,, *Church growth Principles: Separating Fact from Fiction* (Nashville, TN: Broadman Press, 1981), pg. 21.

13 Hadaway, pg. 27.

often do not, because prospects are not visited quickly."14 visitation and assimilation are the keys to translating a one day surge in attendance into growth. Visits to prospects can be made weekly and should continue for several additional weeks and even months.

In chapter seven, Hadaway makes a very important statement: A church must be able to attract a steady stream of visitors because only a small percentage of those who visit will eventually join; and because this is a very mobile society, a regular of additions is necessary in order for churches just to stay even and avoid decline--much less start growing."15

Hadaway places emphasis on the fact that it has been consistently proven that the greatest source of finding, bringing, and keeping visitors is from the members themselves. He states,

> "almost every book on Church Growth which mentions the major of new-members quotes research concerning the percentage of new members who joined or first-visited because of an invitation from a friend or family member."16

---

14 Hadaway, pg. 27.

15 Hadaway, pg. 125-126.

16 Hadaway, pg. 125.

The results appear so consistent that it is safe to say that a majority of people attend a church for the first-time due to this sort of invitation.

In Lyle E. Schaller's <u>44 ways to Increase Church Attendance</u> every chapter is full of ideas and techniques in increasing and attracting visitors. Chapter two offered more information regarding the topic of this dissertation.

Chapter two covers expanding from a single service on Sunday to two or more services. The idea of going to multiple services on Sunday will automatically increase the number of visitors coming church. Most churches that have been used to a single traditional service might and will resist the concept to a single traditional service might and will resist the concept of multiple services on a Sunday.

In fact, a good reason to add multiple services is that if the church is too traditional for the incoming visitors and the surrounding community, which could happen if the church has been ingrown for a number of years and the community has undergone a cultural change, the traditional service can continue with its respective custom and songs while the visitors are joined by regular members that desire to see the church grow. While the traditional service continues in its own ways, the new service can be tailored toward a more contemporary setting, a new hour, and new goals for growth. This in turn would cause the church to concentrate on creating a new and altogether different congregation.

> Schaller expresses the idea thus:
> "The central reason for such a proposal, rather than to attempt to combine unchurched people into a long established congregation, is that the majority of adults are more receptive to a request to help pioneer some new rather than to respond to an invitation to join an ongoing and often exclusionary group." 17

It is very interesting to read the many examples of how church members and leaders can be the agents which teach members how to act toward visitors.

Herb Miller in his book How To Build a Magnetic Church gives an example that is so common in churches. The title of this example is "Warmth in the Pulpit." He gives a bird's eye view of how easy it is to remain distant from a new visitor and cause an impression of you-are-not-wanted to them.

---

17 Lyle E. Schaller, 44 Ways to Increase Church Attendance (Nashville, TN: Abingdon, Press, 1988), pg. 52

The story reads:

> "A woman in a declining church wrote on a consultant's data-gathering sheet: 'a family that is shopping for a church home has visited our church a couple of times. I was behind them in line after the service when they reached the pastor. He turned away and was talking with someone over in the coat room-with his hand limply extended to these visitors. He never did acknowledge their presence. Would you choose this as your new church?"18

Miller goes to state that this was not an isolated incident, but something the entire church membership did because people tend to take on the attitude, style and behavior modeled by their leaders. Miller continues throughout his book to give examples on how to remove those things that keep a church from being vibrant and magnetic. He gives nine secrets that make a church magnetic from being vibrant and magnetic.

A great book to use as a guide in learning where the souls of the unchurched are in their lives is the book **The Contagious Congregation** by George O. Hunter III. The author of this book states that the place to begin effective witnessing is with human motives.

---

18 Herb Miller, (Nashville,TN: Abingdon, Press, 1987), 65.

"Effective communication of the Gospel begins with a demonstration of its relevance."[19] Hunter quotes England's Donald Lord Soper, "We must begin where people are, rather where we would like them to be."[20] Hunter believes that the point of contact between people and the Gospel is people's needs, hopes, yearnings, fears, longings, and deepest motives. Never before has it been so clear that human beings have so many motives. Christianity must be armed with the full, powerful Gospel to meet every basic need which humans exemplify in their lives.

Hunter states: "The evangelizer's job is to find the theater battle, to fashion a battle plan, and marshal the appropriate Christian resources for the engagement."[21] Hunter uses Maslow's Hierarchy of Human Motives model to help his listeners understand where the unchurched need help in life. If the evangelizer or church member can learn Maslow's Hierarchy of Human Needs, he will know what and how to meet those needs. The Evangelizer will present Jesus Christ as the Jehova-Jirah for that need.

---

19 George G. Hunter III, The Contagious Congregation (Nashville, TN: Abingdon Press, 1979), pg. 39.

20 Hunter III., Pg. 39.

21 Hunter III., Pg. 40.

Another interesting point in Hunter's book has to do with communicating the Gospel to resistant secular people. This chapter is very interesting because many church members feel that they have to wait for souls to walk-in on their own to church, and it has been a proven fact that this rarely happens. As stated before, a church must be intentional in its seeking of the unchurched if it desires to increase its membership.

The average church is going to have to teach members how to become intentional in their approach to those who do not know Christ as their Lord. Undoubtedly in their search for unchurched people, the church members will encounter a person resistant to the Gospel. As a result the church members will either discontinue reaching those people or prepare themselves for a long and patient teaching of Christ to this seemingly resistant hearer.

Hunter gives five areas which have suffered secularization and are in dire need of evangelical relief. The first is ignorance and it is the Gospel of Jesus Christ which has the power to remove ignorance and place instead knowledge and truth. The second is death; again the Gospel can present life in Jesus.

The is third is guilt from a life embedded with sin, and the Gospel is the answer for this dilemma. The fourth is doubt--once again doubt can only be remedied by faith in Jesus. The final area is belonging. Today's three greatest fears are belonging, safety, and not being loved. These three fears have gripped many people not know Christ, leaving them feeling devastated in their lives.

DESIGN OF THE STUDY

This dissertation is written with the intent that it will become a book. It will consist of two parts. Part one will consist of the idea of attraction of visitors in these trying times of the church. Part two will address concerns and issues in retaining visitors first visit to the church. Jesus indicated that the church can do great work when He said, "He that believes on me, the works that I do shall he do also; and greater works these shall he do; because I go unto my Father." [22]

In another passage Christ told His disciples, "But you shall receive power, after that the Holy Ghost is come upon you: and you shall be witnesses unto me both in Jerusalem, and in all Judea, and in Samaria, and unto the

---

[22] Gospel of John 14:12, The works of Christ, his followers will do.

Uttermost part of the earth."[23] The greatest quest for any church is to' be able to attract the lost and process them into mature Christian adults who will continue to attract and reach those around them who are lost.

Developing a workable plan of attracting and retaining visitors is the issue that this book attempts to address. There are very few books written on visitor retention. One of the reasons for this is, of course, the tremendous work and effort placed in evangelistic programs and in incorporating and assimilating the new converts. In the past evangelistic programs have helped reach lost people with I wide range of approaches. How ever today's harvest must be met in their hour of need. The style and mechanisms to reach today's lost souls will not be successful if done by direct approaches. It is this writer's opinion that the first line of evangelists who encounter the lost will be men and women who practice the Andrew and Barnabas ministries.

The ministry of Andrew is evangelism. He worked specifically to bring the lost to Christ. In John's Gospel, Andrew is the disciple who heard John the Baptist speak of Jesus as the Lamb of God.[24] After following Jesus, he

---

[23] Acts 1:8, Conversation with Christ on reaching the world.

[24] The Gospel of John 1:29, John the Baptist-the lamb of God.

Left to go find Simon Peter his brother and bring him to Jesus. The Andrew ministry is those members of a congregation who go out of their way to attract visitors to their church.

The ministry of Barnabas, too, is evangelistic, but the emphasis on building friendships. In the book of Acts, Barnabas is found diligently working to organize and connect visitor with converts. In Acts 4:36-37, Barnabas is the son of consolation, who having land, sold it and brought the money to the church. He is a giver and sharer. In Acts 9:26,27, Barnabas is viewed as a co-worker oriented, which is why Barnabas took Saul and brought him to the apostles. In Acts 11:21, Barnabas is a servant leader; in 11:25,26, he is a goal achiever; a helper in 11:29,30, and an encourager in 15:39. The ministry of Barnabas can be viewed as that ministry which, through building relationships, helps retain visitors who come to church.

It is the conclusion of this writer that there is a need for popular treatment, constructed from a biblical outline, with contemporary demographic supplementary material taken from Hispanic churches to help in application. In addition, most of the books written are for leaders interested in church growth. This book will be constructed for the English reader at first, but in time, it will be translated into Spanish for the Hispanic pastor and leaders. All pertinent data for this project will be taken strictly from Hispanic churches, thus giving the Spanish readers better to the material found in this book.

READER'S NOTES

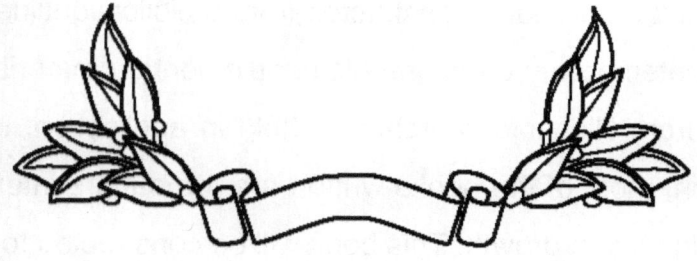

CHAPTER ONE
CONCEPT OF ATTRACTION

Recently I had the privilege of working with an established church in the San Bernardino, California area. The pastor, a good friend of mine, had asked me to help train his congregational members in the area of evangelism. Two years before this invitation, the church membership celebrated their 75th year in existence. For a long time, this church had been survived by mostly elderly people until this new pastor came in and started moving the church toward growth. Before the arrival of the new pastor, the church had been given the name "the Ben Gay congregation."

The church was in dire need of a visitor attraction and retention transfusion. At the beginning of a Sunday evening service, I was at the back of the church by the main entrance doors. Three young women with infants and children came in, and we quickly moved to accommodate them in one of the rear benches where there was only one other older member sitting. The usher waved his hand in a motion for the three women to sit in this row. The older member sitting on the bench stood up for these women to squeeze by but they were unable to do so. There was very little room left between benches, due to recent remodeling completed to create maximum room for more benches. The older member was then told to move to the end of the row toward the Window. The older member gathered his two bundles that were on top of the bench (taking up valuable sitting room) and moved over about one person space. He then turned around to see if the one space given was enough, and noticed that more room was needed. He then expressed some frustration in having to move again. It was at this point that two of the visitors were able to sit down, squashed together, contending with their children still standing between them and the pew in front, blocking their view of what was happening on the platform. The older member was struggling to listen to what was happening on the platform. He was bothered by the shuffling and noise being created by the visitors and their children as they struggled to accommodate themselves also. It never dawned on the older member that if the bundles were placed on the floor underneath the bench in front of him that more room would be created where everybody could sit comfortably.

Finally, one of the ushers saw the problem and asked the older member to please place the bundles underneath the bench so that everybody could sit better. The member reluctantly obeyed, and the problem was resolved.

In a setting where church membership is not encouraged or required to be intentionally sensitive to visitors, the problem of how to attract and retain visitors becomes critical. In the Hispanic culture as in others, people who seek a church on their own are usually on their last attempt to finding a solution or answer for their pain or suffering. These people are hurting so deeply that they are seeking any kind of a solution to their dilemma. The numbers of people seeking a church are usually too small in comparison with the numbers a church needs to keep growing. Thus, the problem of finding and attracting visitors for any church crucial for the long-term health of the congregation. Having incidents like the example mentioned above can kill any chance a church has in trying to attract and retain visitors.

Kirk Hadaway writes:
> A church must be able to attract a steady stream of visitors because only a small percentage of those who visit will eventually join; and because this is a very mobile society, a regular supply of additions is necessary in order for churches just to stay even and avoid decline-much less to start growing.[1]

A church grows by three means. The first is called biological growth, i.e., via the birth of babies into the fold of the church.

---
[1] C. Kirk Hadaway, church Growth Principles: Separating Fact from Fiction (Nashville, TN: Broadman Press, 1991), pg. 125.

The second method is called transfer growth. This is the growth that usually happens when people move from church to church. The third method is called new convert growth. This is the method of bringing new members into a church through evangelism.

Other than through biological growth, it is important that a church learn how to attract new visitors. What may attract one person or family may not necessarily attract another person or family. What may attract people from one culture may not necessarily attract those from another culture. Herein lies the dilemma of developing a workable plan of attracting and retaining visitors. Too often in the past, churches have targeted one culture, or type of people to ensure church growth.

In larger cities today, many communities with mixed cultures and peoples are developing. All one has to do is drive around to tile various ethnic sections of some of the larger cities to see how these areas are growing. Most large cities in America have undergone cultural changes. For example, the city of Los Angeles was originally populated with Hispanics and Indians. Today it has one of the fastest growing Asian communities in America. In fact, on the Pomona 60 freeway. One can see three and distant shopping malls very close by:

La Puente Hills mall, the Oriental shopping mall, and across the freeway many Hispanic shops and restaurants. Even planned communities are catering to selected people in regard to age, status of life, or wealth. Older and more established residential areas are undergoing cultural changes as younger people move away from home and their parents retire to other ares. There is no guarantee that a church will find the culture or even the kind of people it desires to attract in sufficient numbers to allow the church to continue growing.

Concept of visitor attraction and retention

The concept of visitor attraction and retention is associated with understanding some vital principles in both the perspective of the church and the perspective of the people it is trying to attract. The way the church used to attract people in the 50's cannot be compared to methods used in the 90's. The profile of the people in general in the 50's were much more friendly and neighborly.

In the 90's, people in general purposefully seek isolation the point of alienating themselves from the rest of the world. the fast pace and constant change of the current society causes people to spend more time alone or with their immediate families.

Joe Aldrich, author of the book Life-Style Evangelism, puts it this way:

> Let's consider some reasons why we appear "ineffective" when compared to the apostles. Our purpose is not to excuse ourselves. But clearly we need to understand some of the forces or influences which hinder our effectiveness.
>
> First, the need to relate to the ever-changing number of people in our daily experience has crippled our ability to relate effectively to even one person. Excessive relational demands have crippled our relational capacities. There are simply too many people. A casual stroll down the street brings me face to face with dozens of people every minute. I cannot possibly recognize or relate to them. I must pass by them and treat them as indifferently as parts of machinery moving down an assembly line. To make matters worse, population densities of most metropolitan areas reinforce alienation and indifference.
>
> This attitude of isolation becomes a way of life this response of unconcern may be necessary to maintain some sort of psychological equilibrium. But it certainly hurts the evangelistic enterprise. At the times when relationship is critical to the gospel's impact, we discover that most Christians have neither significant contacts with non-Christians nor the ability to relate in a redemptive manner. When it comes to relating to people, we find that bigness is not necessarily best. [2]

---

[2] Joseph C. Aldrich, Life Style Evangelism (Portland, OR: MultnomaPress, 1981), 16,17.

This phenomenon began in the western world after the great technological and political revolutions of the present century. Man freed himself from the rigidity of the former social orders; but in doing so, he cut himself loose from all that tied him to a world with stable relationships. Today, man is often a stranger to himself, as he is with other people. Man feels lost and unable to return to the more simple ways of life that his parents enjoyed. Add to this feeling of alienation and isolation the emerging needs in society for man to blend and work with people from other cultures and communities and the result is people crossing cultural barriers with little or no understanding of each other's values and needs. In many of this nation's major and minor cities, there is an array of cultures, values, and needs of people congregating in clusters all around. Mankind must interrelate with different cultures in order to do business day to day.

In the average church, members of congregations are resisting the idea of intercultural relationships. The resistance is usually internal, but can be noticeable in cultures that are at the opposite end of the spectrum. With the continual influx of new and ethnic groups into the United States, the church will continue to struggle to educate its members who resist the idea of accepting other people into their fold.

If the whole church is blind to this problem then the ability to attract and retain new visitors will diminish to the point of losing its calling of sinners merely to protect itself from intercultural diversity. This resistance has forced many churches to die of old age and other diverse diseases. It has caused the church to remain isolated and has diminished its strength of reaching the world for Christ.

This is what the concept of visitor attraction and retention concerns. It seeks to develop a workable plan of attracting and retaining visitors by helping churches understand some basic, yet vital principles. The principles relate to perception. The first principle is the perception the church has to its biblical mandates. The perception that the church has of itself and its call can either help her succeed with its mission or prevent the spread of the Gospel and the growth of the church.

The second principle applies to the perception which the community has towards the church. If the people within the community ministry area have a poor view of the church, they will not visit the church. Every church has a unique community ministry area to which the Holy Spirit desires to minister. A church cannot be of one mind of only surviving, but of excelling in reaching the lost. The challenge of the church is going to be in the area of overcoming the obstacles that hinder her. Only by going beyond its normal ministry area and seeking out those lost segments of people will the church experience the satisfaction of responding to its call. By expanding its outreach to other kinds of people-groups, the church will excel in growth.

The third principle deals with the perception the church has toward the community. Though desiring to grow in membership, the church wants to stay within its own culture. Finding those who need to be ministered to different from those in the church often stops churches from evangelizing them. The outreach embarked outside of their ministry area will yield very little growth and alienate the surrounding community, which is the area the Holy Spirit intended the church to reach with the Gospel.

If the church had been obedient to the leading of the Holy Spirit, it would have fulfilled a vital mission that God had intended for all His churches. The community that is being spoken of here is that segment of society that has been abandon by all. It encompasses everyone from drunks to homeless people, and gang members to drug addicts. It also includes orphans, single parents, blended families, mixed marriages, and all categories of people who traditionally have not been accepted.

These three principles are the reasons why churches have experienced introversion and have become ingrown.

John Miller in his book <u>Outgrowing the Ingrown Church,</u> states:

> "From my own experiences as a pastor and church member, I had a rather firm grasp on the essential features of the ingrown church; I discerned that these qualities were in some degree deviations from the norm of the New Testament church. But before this I had not clearly seen that the introverted church reflected members' unbelieving resistance to the will of the king, as expressed by His missionary mandate. After Spain I saw the introverted church no longer as partly out of line with the divine will, but radically disobedient to it. At the same time I realized that the ingrown church was missing out in respect to the Lord's missionary presence, which enables congregations to fulfill the Great Commission."[3]

Curry W. Mavis viewed a similar problem in the church, and in his book: <u>Advancing the smaller Church</u> he Writes:

> "Like persons, local churches are sometimes introverted. Following the introverted pattern in human personality, these churches turn their interests and their energies inwardly upon themselves. They are concerned primarily with their own affairs. Sometimes they devote most of their attention to spiritual Introspection which results in a neglect of spiritual

---

[3] John C. Miller, <u>Outgrowing the Ingrown Church</u> (Grand Rapids, MI: Zondervan Publishing House, 1986), 27, 28.

expression in their communities. 4

Outgrown churches have learned how to overcome this introversion, which has allowed them to become large churches. The mandate of Matthew 28:19, Mark 16:15, and Acts 1:8 of going into the whole world outweighs any traditions, sentiments and cultural barriers that hinder growth.

Churches which refuse to change with the community's needs and resist attracting visitors from a cultural changing environment will become ingrown. Churches which do change with the needs of their communities will become outgrown. The difference in perception between outgrown and ingrown behavior the member can blind churches in their abilities to attract and retain visitors. Outgrown churches take every possible advantage in the makeup of societal differences and behaviors to attract and retain visitors, and thus have an opportunity to witness and reach those people who are lost.

Churches which are ingrown take every opportunity to avoid contact with societies that are different from them, receding into their four walls, and hiding away from change.

---

4 Curry W. Mavis, <u>Advancing The Smaller Church</u> (Grand Rapids. MI: Zondervan Publishing house. 1957), 30.

Frank R. Tillapaugh in his book <u>Unleashing the Church:</u> calls this approach "The Fortress Mentality."[5] He sees the same thing in the membership of many churches, a mentality of staying within the fort for protection as the soldiers did from the Indians in the Old West.

Communities which have undergone cultural changes must face the incoming culture or subculture in order to manage it. Leaders of communities as well as merchants and businesses must encounter head on the problems presented by this diversity of cultures. The problems are not going to go away with time. They must be worked through at all costs. The church in general must do likewise if they intend to make a difference in their communities and the kingdom of God.

The struggle of the ingrown churches to survive will become greater and greater with each passing year. As their membership continues to move away from the area, they will find it very difficult to continue finding new sources of people to attract. The members who have moved away will also find it difficult to return to the church in the old neighborhood. The difficulty will become increasingly

---

[5] Frank Tillapaugh, <u>Unleashing the Church</u> (Ventura CA: Regal Books, 1978), Pg. 8

Intolerable to point that the members will find a different church closer to where they now live. If this process continues, the church will dwindle in numbers and eventually die.

In attracting new converts, a church must evaluate the mandate that the Word of God has placed on it. Why is this evaluation important? The importance of the mandate will override the traditions and cultural limitations the church has placed on itself. Many times a church will become ingrown because its traditions and cultural limitations outweigh the mandate of reaching out to the diverse people within. When a church reaches the conclusion that evangelism is more important than traditions and regulations, it will seek new ways of attracting and retaining the people that it reaches.

The church must also evaluate its profile and the sensitivity of its people. It must begin to teach its recipients to become more sensitive to others who are not like them. Its members must learn new ways of expressing to different people their love and compassion for the lost. When an ingrown church accomplishes this task, the church is able to face the world as a servant. The church will demonstrate the incarnate Christ to its visitors and thus fulfill its destiny as a church.

The congregation will be encouraged to invite new prospects to church if they have an idea what people in the community need. Church officials, leaders, and pastors must have a fairly good understanding of what changes are happening in the world and how these changes are affecting people. A church that knows the needs of the people in its community is a church that reaches souls. At least half of the programs in a church should be geared toward community needs. The congregation should be made aware of any and all programs and activities the church has to offer visitors. The congregation needs to be trained and equipped with the knowledge of making visitors feel welcomed and lovingly received when they visit the church every time.

SUMMARY

We live in a time in which many biblical prophecies may come to pass. Add to that idea that a great diversity of ethnic people groups live in areas all around us and we have within our grasp very powerful elements that can help in reaching out, not just to our own culture, but to nearly every culture in the world. For the person whose life is filled with the love of Jesus, this can only translate to evangelism. The Hispanic church has within its culture the ability to create an atmosphere of love, music, friendliness, and joyful noise unto God that could literally attract many, diverse ethnic groups to know Jesus as their personal Savior. The next chapter will deal with the concept of heritage, and what the generations of today are having to wrestle with to attract and retain visitors.

READER'S NOTES

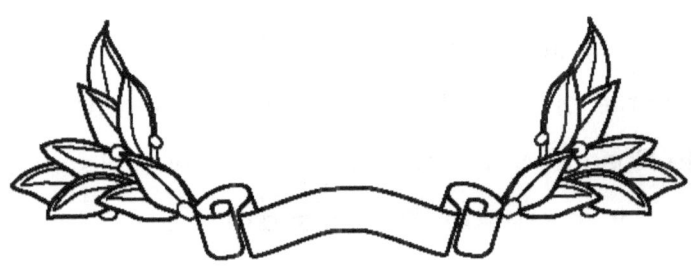

CHAPTER TWO
HERITAGE

HISTORY OF THE DEVELOPMENT
Of THE HISPANIC CHURCH

The Hispanic church is rooted in several branches of Christendom. It is believed, though, that most of the Hispanic branches came from the Holiness Movement in Methodism. It is also believed, for the most part, that some of the Hispanic branches came from their English counterparts sometime after the 1920's. For example, the "Asamblea de Dios," a Hispanic organization formed in 1914, came from its English counterpart the Assemblies of God. The "Asamblea Apostolica de la fe en Cristo Jesus Inc." organized itself from men that had been converted through such pastors like William J. C. Seymour, a black preacher from the Apostolic Mission on Azusa Street in the city of Azusa, California. A couple by the name of Abunio Lopez and is wife Rosa were one of the first known Hispanics converted to this new movement in a revival by Seymour around 1906. Later came a man by the name of Frank Bartleman in 1909 and baptized his wife Rosa who was one of the first known Hispanics converted to this new movement and revival by Seymour around 1906. Later came a man by the name of Frank Bartleman in 1909 and baptized Luis Lopez, who in turn baptized Juan Avarro and Francisco Llorente. Around 1906-1912 the Lord called Brother Llorente to develop many of today's hymns for the Hispanic church in Los Angeles. Brother Llorente was used by the Lord to reach another young man by the name of Antonio Castaneda Nava who became the first presiding president of the newly organized Apostolic Assembly in the Faith of Christ Jesus. Many other branches of Hispanic churches came from the Pentecostal Assemblies of the World, Inc., which is a black, English speaking, Jesus Name holiness movement.

Many of these Hispanic movements took their methodology of reaching the lost from their English counterparts or the mother churches from which they came. Even their styles of dress and forms of worship were borrowed, for they knew nothing else. For example, the women auxiliary group of the Asamblea de la fe en Cristo Jesus Inc., known today as the "Sociadad Femenil de Dorcas," Wore hats in their early years. Today they wear veils to cover their heads, according to 1 Corinthians 11. The head covering for women was understood because of their translation of Scripture in the Spanish version, but the kind of covering was borrowed from the black women of the Pentecostal Assemblies of the World, Inc. Later, the Apostolic Assembly decided to revert to the veil instead of the hat for the covering of their women in keeping more closely with Old Testament culture.

There seemed to be a great need for some of these Hispanic assemblies to develop their form of structure and governing laws before they developed their religious and evangelistic methods. The reason is that the religious and evangelistic methods borrowed from their English counterparts were working fine at that time. Also, in an institutional sense, they saw that the local churches had the responsibility to develop whatever worked better in each church. The rapid form and structure of the assemblies eventually outweighed the local church's decisions and responsibilities to conduct outreach away from the local ministry areas.

As the governmental structure of an assembly gets to be top heavy, its need to survive begins to demand from the local churches strict adherence to its by-laws. This, in turn, creates a vacuum in local churches in the area of resources, personnel, finances, and time. The super structure of an assembly of churches then works from the top down instead of the bottom up. That is, the super structure creates programs and activities for its own survival, instead of meeting the the needs of the local church to reach the lost. This is, of course, similar to what happened to Christ His disciples when they were working on a Sabbath to feed themselves. When Christ was asked why His disciples were working on a Sabbath, Christ responded that "the Sabbath was for man, not man for the Sabbath."[1] The law of the Sabbath was made to help man, not enslave him.

This type of super structure develops only with religious organizations that are organized as corporations or similar governmental systems. Assemblies that are associated by other means with their local churches and are independent do not necessarily have these types of problems. The primary reason for this is due to the fact that independent local churches retain their autonomy of government. On the other hand, when churches mature and lose sight of their biblical mandates, they begin to slide into legalism and into what Richard Gazowsky mentions in his book, "Just Add Water" He states:

---

[1] Matthew 12:1-8, Jesus disciples worked on the Sabbath for food.

> "Most organizations are inherently tribal in their structure. Most of the shared behavior between people in that organization is called "Culture," Culture is really a feel-good tool, a set of behavioral blinders. It makes a company or church feel comfortable with its habits. In the case of a church, if its tenets are in place over a long period of time, they become 'belief system' even longer, and then mature into doctrines of "heaven or hell" issues. If the tribal-church culture goes unchanged, it will even begin to reject newcomers that do not understand its significances." 2

The reason for this information is to help the reader understand why some churches have success in the area of evangelism and others do not. There are many reasons why churches do not grow, yet the main reason seems to be because members stop bringing or inviting visitors to church. A significant way to cripple a church from growing is to stop inviting or bringing visitors. Nothing cripples a church faster than to see it Sunday after Sunday without any new souls listening to the Gospel.

The mandate of Matthew 28: 19,20 is to go into all nations and preach the Gospel, teach, and make disciples. It is not the building of super structures that the mandate stresses, but sending men and women out and make disciples of nations.

---
2 Richard Gazowsky, <u>Just Add Water</u> (San Francisco, CA: Voice of Pentecost, 1992), pgs. 178, 179.

The Current State of the Hispanic Church

How can small Hispanic churches attract and retain visitors? In the 1950's Hispanic Pentecostal churches were on the upswing numerically. They were primarily fast-paced churches dynamic music and popular, people-oriented styles of worship. The churches were evangelistically aggressive. However, in last few decades, the Pentecostal churches have passed through what has been called "The Sociological Cycle" and will no doubt pass through all the levels through which other denominations have gone. 3 Towns describes the Sociological Cycle of four stages that denominations grow through in time.

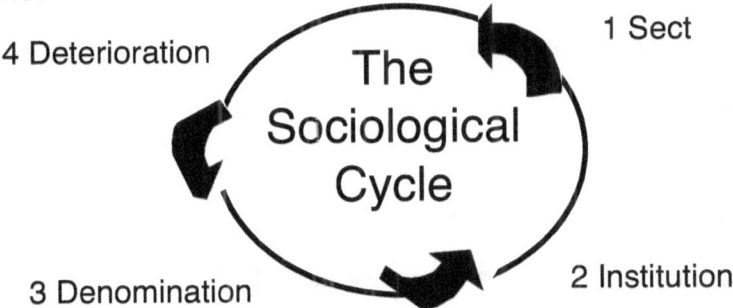

Fig. 3. The above diagram is taken from Towns' book, **America's Fastest Growing Churches.**

---

3 Elmer L. Towns, America's Fastest Growing Churches (Nashville, TN.: Impact Books, 1972), pg. 156.

The first cycle is known as a sect: a group-organized, ecclesiastical body: way of life, class of persons; a dissenting or schismatic religious body; a religious denomination. Once started, it quickly moves to the second cycle, the institution or organization phase. The third cycle is the denomination, and the fourth cycle is Deterioration.

Originally, the Pentecostal movement was viewed as a sect, but recently it has moved toward the third stage, denomination. The Pentecostal movement in the United States, along with other post Pentecostal movements such as the Apostolic Assemblies, United Apostolic or Pentecostal denominations, which strictly Jesus Name movements, are today experiencing the second and, in some cases, the third stage of the Sociological Cycle. They are not the only ones who have had a problem in moving through these areas. Most Trinitarian movements that have organized into some structure of an assembly or denomination have experienced the same problems. Some of these movements have become entrenched in the second or institutional stage or level, still others have gone on through the entire Sociological Cycle.

In the late 1920's a German philosopher-sociologist by name of Ernst Troeltsch originally wrote about the churches that grow from a sect status to ecclesia/assembly, or what today would be termed the denomination stage. Troeltsch's model begins as a sect and then moves to become an institution. It then moves to the stage of a fully organized ecclesia/assembly, and finally will end at the deterioration stage.

Troeltsch's model and cycle of growth is also known by other names. For example, the first or 'sect' stage has been termed the fundamentalism stage. The second stage of this cycle has been label 'institution.' The third stage is known as a 'denomination' and the final cycle is 'theological liberalism.' Some even combine denomination and theological liberalism together in the same stage.

A partial example of the organization stage is found in the book of Acts. Chapter 11 and verses 19-26 can help in understanding the development of the first two stages of Troeltsch's model.

> "Now they which were scattered abroad upon the persecution that arose about Stephen traveled as far as Phoenicia, and Cyprus, and Antioch, preaching the word to none but the Jews only. And some of them were men of Cyprus and Cyrene, which, when they were come to Antioch, spoke unto the Grecians, preaching the Lord Jesus. And the hand of the Lord was with them: and a great number believed, and turned unto the Lord. Then the tidings of these things came unto the ears of the church which was in Jerusalem: and they sent for Barnabas, that he should go as far as Antioch. Who, when he came,

and had seen the grace of God, was glad, and exhorted them all, that with purpose of heart they would cleave unto the Lord . . . Then departed Barnabas to Tarsus, for to seek Saul: And when he had found him, he brought him unto Antioch."4

This incident in the book of the Acts demonstrates how the church was born in the city of Antioch. Stephen's persecution and death caused many to flee Jerusalem into other parts or the then known world. Wherever these men fled, they took with them the Gospel of the Lord Jesus Christ. The city of Antioch is example. Men from Cyprus and Cyrene came to the city of Antioch and there preached the Gospel of Jesus to its inhabits. As they preached, "the hand of the Lord was with them and great number believed, and turned unto the Lord."5

READER'S NOTES

---

4 Acts 11:19-26, Barnabas is sent to Antioch to organize the church.

5 Acts 11:21, The hand of the Lord is with the men of Cyrus and Cyrene

PARTIAL SOCIOLOGICAL CYCLE VIEW OF THE CHURCH IN ANTIOCH

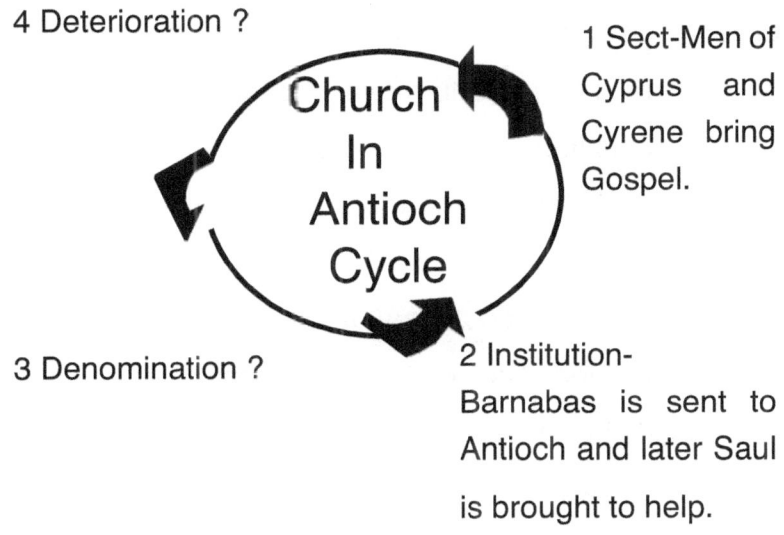

Fig. 4. The above diagram is taken from Towns' book, **America's Fastest Growing Churches.**

> When the news got back to Jerusalem, the apostles decided to send Barnabas to investigate and help the work in the city of Antioch. When Barnabas arrived in Antioch, "and had seen the grace of God, was glad, and exhorted them all, that with purpose of heart they would cleave unto the Lord."6

Barnabas knew that the work needed to be done in Antioch was more than he could do alone. He decided to

---

6 Acts 11:21, The hand of the Lord is with the men of Cyrus and Cyrene.

go to Tarsus to find Saul and bring him to help in the organization of the church of Antioch.

This mentioned passage in Acts is an example of Troeltsch's model existing In the beginning of church development. The need to move through the cycle from point to point is found in all levels of the church: in the local church, a department in the church, as well as in an assembly of churches.

Today the institutional stage is called by many the organizational stage. The need of the organizational stage is what builds the infrastructure of a church, organization, or denomination and allows the infrastructure to develop the government (rules, guidelines, constitution, and officers). This in turn forces the denominational stage to begin to process itself.

In the organizational stage, the infrastructure allows pastors of local churches of the organization to share authority with the organization leaders to achieve the work and ministry in a greater scale than that of the local alone. The authority and power is partially shared, and a balance is achieved because at this stage of the organization, its leaders are also the pastors of local churches within the organization. The duties and work of the congregation are not sufficient to warrant them to be full time;

insufficient income also hinders full time status. It is at this point that a need for more and better guidelines is required to develop stronger language and stricter adherence to the guidelines of an earlier writ or constitution. Successive waves of amendments will follow until the need for full authority and power over the local churches creates a radical shift in this type of government.

The dynamic tension between the organizational and denominational stages causes the inversion of power, freedom, strength, and resources of local churches to the organization's infrastructure.

Reader's Notes

EARLY STRUCTURE OF POWER DISPLAYED AT THE ORGANIZATIONAL STAGE

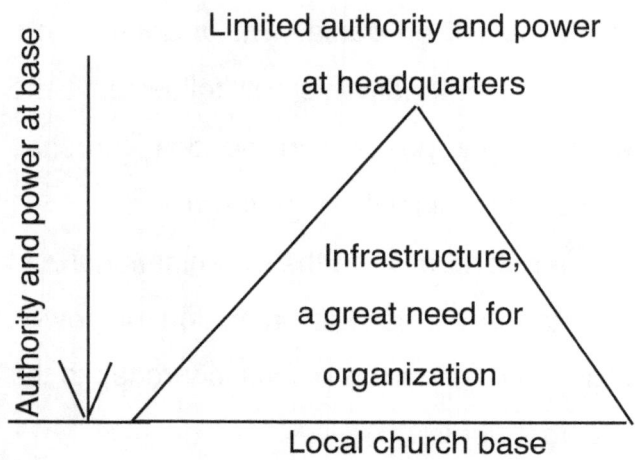

Fig. 5. The above diagram is extended to maintain continuity of thought and illustrated by author.

The upside down triangle in the next page displays how power and authority is inverted by the leaders of the organization. The power and authority is radically shifted from the local church level to the top or the organization permanently and exclusively. The leaders, for the most part, do not hold both a pastorate and an organizational leadership position. It is generally too difficult to do both When the leadership at the top of the organization triangle ceases to have its fingers at the pulse of the needs of the local churches, it is then that the organization begins to have tension and stress with the local churches.

LATER STRUCTURE OF POWER SHIFT IN THE ORGANIZATIONAL STAGE

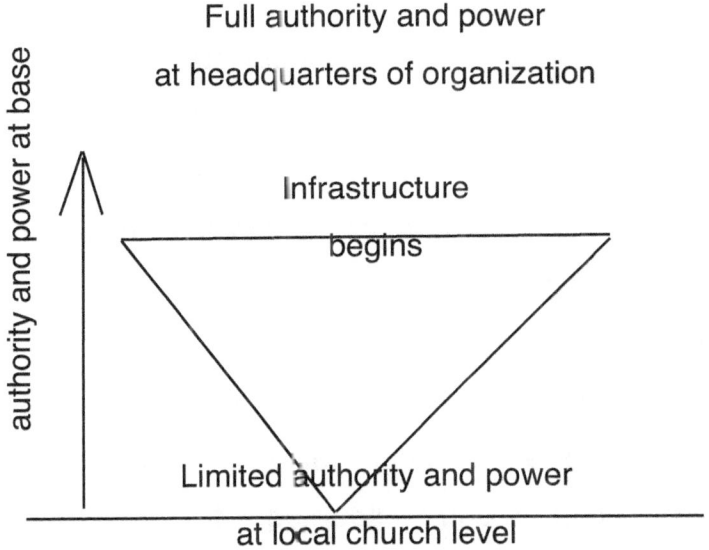

Fig. 6 The above diagram is extended from previous models to maintain continuity of thought and is illustrated by author.

Leaders at this level have discovered that in order to manage the institutional stage effectively, all power must be at the helm. A total and complete transfer of power from local churches to the headquarters means that local churches will be told what and how much they can do at the local level of the church.

The radical shift of power with the inversion of the the church. The radical shift of power with the inversion of the authority causes the local church to re-evaluate its priorities, due to its constant draining of resources. The local church needs to understand these two points of importance in the development of Troeltsch's Sociological Cycle Model. These two points are, of course, between the cycles of sect and institution, and institution and denomination. To better explain the problems that arise between these critical points in the Hispanic churches, David O. Moberg's model of the differences between the church and a social institution should be investigated.

David Moberg, a church sociologist from Marquette University, has developed his own cycle. He sees a "process by which cults originate, develop into sects, and then change into denomination, perhaps finally to emerge from the process as churches."[7]

---

[7] David O. Moberg, The Church or a Social Institution (Englewood Cliffs, NJ;Prentice-Hall, Inc. , 1962), pg. 100.

DAVID MOBERG'S SOCIOLOGICAL CYCLE MODEL

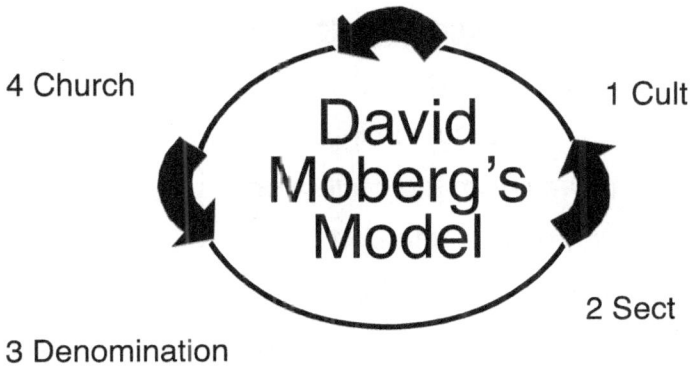

Fig. 7. The above diagram is extended from previous models to maintain continuity of thought and is illustrated by author.

David Moberg's model can help explain the two points of importance in the development cycle. Most-cult-like churches that have undergone Moberg's cycle can attest to the first stage of cult to sect. Depending on the psychological and theological standing and philosophy of ministry of the Initial cult leaders, the of growth from cult tension of growth from cult sect can be critical one. Throughout church history, there have been cult leaders with psychological and theological standing and philosophy of ministry that did not permit them to grow into a sect. The tension of growth from cult to sect to can be a critical one because the cult leader sees the growth as a present danger to themselves and their cult members. Their belief in themselves and their mission hinder the process. Some cults, where the leadership comes from one man, can have selfish reasons why the cult leader does not desire the cult to continue and develop and will guide the cult away from the cycle process.

The second point of critical importance in the development of Moberg's cycle is between sect and denomination. The critical point develops when the infrastructure needed begins to form in the organization phase. In the organization phase or cycle, the guidelines, rules, and officers are devised and written in some sort of a constitution. This constitution then becomes binding to the point of, in some cases, having more power than Word of God. Depending on the men that develop this constitution and their ability to foresee the needs of future generations, the constitution can become the organization's future worst enemy. This critical point does not seem at first to make any difference, but it is not until three or more generations have functioned under the constitutional tutorage, and all the amendments added by others, that it becomes the noose that slowly chokes the church. When the leader of a cult does not allow their cult to process into a church, they usually end up in a similar situation like that of the Dravidian Branch in Waco, Texas or that of Jim Jones.

According to Elmer Towns, it is the denomination stage that reduces or enhances growth in the local church. Depending makeup of the constitution, either it helps the local churches or it helps the organizational infrastructure. Towns puts it into perspective: "*Liberalism or mainline denominationalism does not have the religious dynamic to naturally attract individuals. When the attendance at denominational-type churches climbs, it does so for extraneous reasons of an external pressure for growth or their spiritual life is void, hence they have no internal dynamic for growth.*"[8]

Elmer Towns is saying in the quote above that the denomination will expect the local church to grow naturally, but will probably not help it grow. Churches in a denomination will grow in attendance only if they do not play by the rules set forth by that de nomination. The reason is that the denomination usually develops its style of organization from either the denomination standards or from the constitution, but not from the experiences of the pastor and leaders who understand the needs of their congregation or community of lost souls.

---

[8] Towns, pg. 157.

Two examples of Elmer Towns' theory are as follows. The first takes place in the city of Whittier, California at the Family Life Center Apostolic Church, whose pastor is David Hernandez, Pastor Hernandez founded that church about twenty-five years ago, and decided to part from the traditional Spanish language that he had grown up with. He started an all-English church to meet the needs of people he felt needed to be ministered in a language other than Spanish. Life-line was created to meet those needs. No one in that area had tried something that bold before. These two elements resulted in him and his church to be viewed as not quite fitting into the denomination.

Another pastor who grew up in the ministry about the same time as that of pastor Hernandez is pastor Adam Lopez of the church in Union City. Pastor Lopez is also quite unique in he, too, grew up in a Hispanic-speaking and worshipping church where his father was the pastor. Pastor Lopez also departed from the traditional ways of conducting church with which he had grown up with and began to minister in a total English setting. Both of these pastors were blessed by God and the churches they have started have become very healthy and vibrant. Their Growth was unprecedented, and their churches functioned. They looked very little like their counterpart pastors of their organization. It is not to say that going all English has caused their success in the Lord, but at the same time something with the language gave them success in attracting and retaining visitors. Spanish churches, on the other hand, have had little success in attracting and retaining visitors and thus growing the church. Today, churches need to rethink their philosophy of ministry to see if it is leading church towards a healthy growth. It must, by it sheer need to evangelize and reach the lost, construct popular programs and activities to bring salvation to those whom the Holy Spirit desires to save.

It is the local church, with its limited resources, that feeds the infrastructure of the denomination with much needed leaders, money, and programs. By using its limited resources and manpower for the denominational needs, the local church restricts and debilitates its own evangelical work. When the local church uses most of its resources in this capacity, it ceases to work to its fullest potential in reaching the lost. The attendance of visitors drops drastically, and so does the growth of the local church. Add to the burden of having limited resources and manpower the demand of the denomination for the pastors and churches to support programs. Services, and other types activities outside the loal church, which squanders, the limited time for the churches to have revivals and increase their visitor attraction and retention, and the result is the crippling effect that denominations cause to local churches. What started once as greatly needed organizational programs, services, and activities can later become the barriers of church growth.

It is a well-known fact that larger denominations do not place total emphasis on reaching the lost because they feel that this is the responsibility of the local church. Its responsibility is to create the infrastructure that allows communication and direction between the local churches and headquarters. Because denominations consider themselves the head of the organization, they can lose perspective and consume the limited resources of the body for their own purposes. When this occurs, the local church is drained of most of its resources. This is the danger that many organized church assemblies are currently facing. There any biblical examples to help in understanding the devastation both Troeltch's and Moberg's models can reach if something is not done.

Two examples will be presented. The first is in Judges 2:7-10:

> "And the people served the Lord all the days of Joshua, and all the days of the elders that outlived Joshua. Who had seen all the great works of the Lord, that he did for Israel.
> And Joshua the son of Nun, the servant of the Lord, died, I a hundred and ten years old ... And also all that generation were gathered unto their fathers: and there arose another generation after them, which knew not the Lord, nor yet the works which he had done for Israel."[9]

Joshua's example of reaching devastation ended with the fourth generation not knowing the Lord of their fathers. It is a dismal situation to see one's grandchildren and great grand-children slowly deteriorate into worshiping pagan gods because there was very little taught to prepare them to acknowledge their need for God. In the next page we will see in a graph 'Joshua's Sociological Cycle model'.

JOSHUA'S SOCIOLOGICAL CYCLE MODEL

---

[9] Judges 2: 7-10, Judges account of four generations.

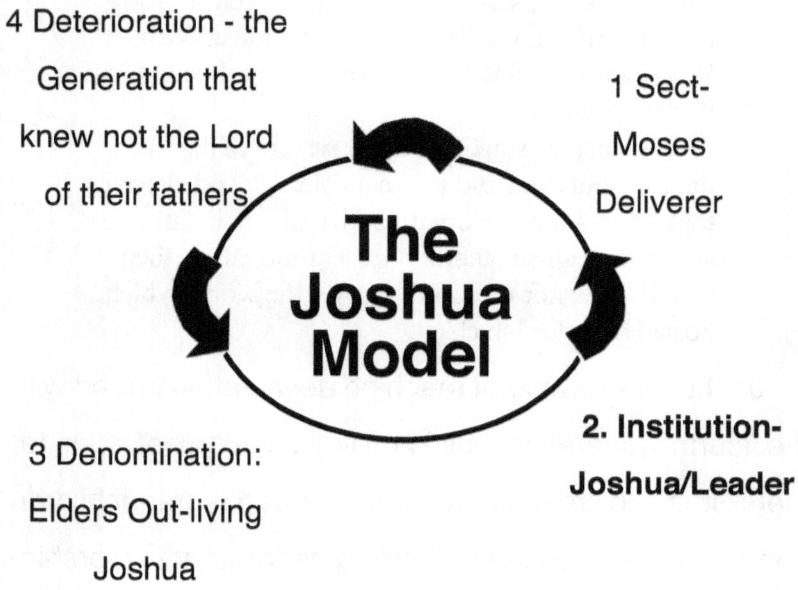

The Joshua Model

4 Deterioration - the Generation that knew not the Lord of their fathers

1 Sect- Moses Deliverer

2. Institution- Joshua/Leader

3 Denomination: Elders Out-living Joshua

Fig. 8. Judges 2:7 -10. Joshua's Model of Four Generations.

Another biblical example is found in 1 Kings 12: I-19. This example is teaching the leaders to seek wisdom from God and not from themselves in greed.

> "And Rehoboam went to Shechem: for all Israel were come to Shechem to make him king. And it came to pass, when Jeroboam the son of Nebat, who was yet in Egypt, heard of it, (for he was fled from the presence of king Solomon, and Jeroboam dwelt in Egypt): That they sent and called him. And Jeroboam and all the congregation of Israel came, and spake unto Rehoboam, saying, thy father made our yoke grievous: now therefore make thou the grievous service of the father, and his heavy yoke which he put upon us, lighter, and we will serve thee

... the king Rehoboam consulted with the old men, that stood before Solomon his father while he yet lived ... But he forsook the counsel of the old men, which they had given him, and consulted with the young men that were grown up with him, and which stood before him ... So Jeroboam and all the people came to Rehoboam the third day, the king had appointed ... and the king answered the people roughly, and forscok the old men's' counsel that they gave him. And spake to them after the counsel of the young men, saying. My father made your yoke heavy, and I will add to your yoke: my father also chastised you with whips, but I will chastise you with scorpions... So Israel rebelled against the house of David unto this day." 10

A balance must be struck by the local churches and the denomination. This balance must favor the local church and not the denomination. The denomination must always remember that its purpose is a global one, whereas the local church is there for the community. The denomination must at all times streamline itself and keep focused on the work it has been called to do, such as he global missionary outreach and the planting of local churches in areas that have not yet been established. The balance between the needs of the denomination and the local church must constantly be evaluated.

---

10 1 Kings 12: 1-19, Rehoboam's decree of the yoke heavier on Israel.

DAVID MOBERG'S SOCIOLOGICAL CYCLE MODEL

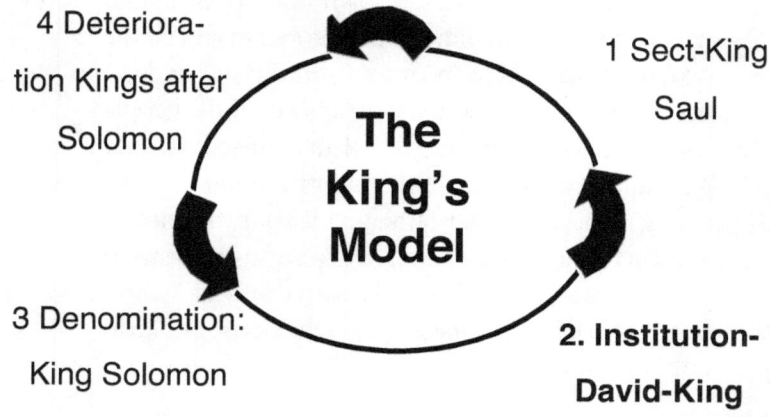

If a balance is not reached, then the disharmony between the local churches and the denomination can cause factions, divisions, and even spawn churches to go independent. The cycles that both Troeltsch and Moberg give of institutional growth can be used to help in understanding what it will take to correct many problems that exist today. Structured organizations will develop to help reach unchurched areas needing missions and evangelist, and use funds and resources there. However, small churches tend to see only the needs they have regarding quality leadership, direction, and vision. The needs of the unchurched will demand that the decision making power be transferred headquarters.

As the needs intensify, the organization will work out some kind of exchange with the small churches to help the organization meet its work load.

Eventually the organization will have to develop a vision statement and goals for all the local churches of the body. This will result in the local churches pooling all of their resources (time, personnel, finances) for the good of the whole organization and not just for the local churches.

If the institutional government persist with its plan without regard to the needs of the local church, it will damage the local church's ability to be an effective agent in that locale. As the local church struggles to meet the challenges of the institutional government, the work to continue reaching the lost will be severely weakened. As the local church loses the battle of reaching the lost, its attendance declines. Eventually the local church will arrive at a mentality of maintenance, where it pays its debt to the super-structure and takes care of what little membership it has. This stalemate will force a regretful condition in the congregation and cause a severe turnover of pastors. This, in turn, will cause small church members to leave their churches in search of bigger ones to meet their needs and those of their children. The downward spiral caused by such circumstances brings eventual death to the church to the church.

Contour of the Hispanic People

In understanding the history of the Hispanic people, one must take into account the diversity of its ethnicity. For example, when the media refers to the nationality of a Mexican, they will use the term Hispanic, because it is a general term that encompasses all branches of Spanish blood.

When the different television programs and talk shows want to address the Hispanic populations, they refer to them Latinos to include the Latin American people. The Latino-based programs, talk shows and soap operas (Novelas) are mainly geared to Latin Americans peoples in such places as Puerto Rico, Cuba, Haiti, Central and Southern American countries. These countries are referred to as Latin American Countries. They depend greatly on programs, talk shows, and soap operas created in the United States.

When referring to people from Mexico, the term to describe these people is Mexicans. It is believed that a ratio of three Mexicans to one Latino enter the U.S. yearly. As one can see, knowing the various terminologies has much to do with understanding which group is being addressed.

Thus, the terminology is very important in understanding the contour of the Hispanic races.

Another very important factor in understanding the terminology to use in the Hispanic races is the amount of time that a generation spends in assimilating with the North American subcultures. Trying to attract and retain any of these people will require knowledge in the generational differences that both time and culture produce.

Every person who leaves his cultural setting and enters another culture will no doubt undergo force changes. These changes bring about new adventures and also stumbling blocks. Anyone who leaves his old culture or country to come to the united States arrives with his own paradigm of how to live. Everything from the foods he eats to the way he dresses, to the way he makes decisions to learning new ways and leaving old ones behind, helps him in one way or another assimilate into his new country. The person who refuses to adapt to his new country's culture or chooses not to adapt because he wishes to go back sooner or later, faces the risk of rejecting it. When the new culture setting is rejected, he will have to find a community where his old values are still being practiced. If he is unable to find such a place, he will undoubtedly return to is homeland.

Mary Ballesteros-Coronel, a reporter of the newspaper La Opinion, wrote an article of a report made from a study by Instituto de Asuntos Publicos de California (PPIC). This study proved that a major part of Mexican immigrants that come into the U.S. return to their native country after only two years of living here and 67% return in five years or less. Belinda Reyes, author of the PPIC study, states that 70% of all Mexicans end up leaving or returning to Mexico permanently after 10 years of living and working in the United States. The Mexicans that return to their native land in less than two years never really intended to stay; they only came for work. Most of these people have little or no education; thus, they can only support work of agricultural and temporal economic level. Mexicans with a higher level of education, possibly the equivalent of high school, are able to find somewhat better jobs in factories or construction, and end up staying here longer. These would be the 67% that will return in an 10 years. These two groups usually have to come into country illegally.

QUESTIONS AND FOOD FOR THOUGHT

What importance does a culture play with people from other countries? How does the culture of the United States help or hinder people of other cultures?

How do people of Spanish cultures assimilate into the United States to become North Americans? These and other questions will be addressed in chapter three.

ACTION STEPS

First and foremost, the Hispanic pastor who wishes to grow the church is responsible for reevaluating the kind of people that have been attracted and converted to membership. This identifies the kind of community that the church has been successful in reaching.

The second step that the Hispanic pastor must research is the community that has been pooled in the past. Does it still offer a large number of possible adherents to warrant the continual investment of resources by the church, i.e., literature, personnel, time, etc .?

The third area that needs to be taken into consideration is the church's resources available to get the job done. Most churches' members do not know how to witness, much less evangelize. The pastor needs to take inventory of who can do what and how much of it. Measures need to be taken to be careful in making sure that the people that will be going out to evangelize are fairly prepared with what they might encounter.

SUMMARY

Having a workable knowledge of the unchurched people around the local church's ministry area will unfailingly aid in attracting and retaining of future members. Understanding the roots of the Hispanic races will assist in understanding how to minister to them. This is why any local church today that wishes to minister to races that have a multiplicity of subcultures must undergo education of the values and needs of the mother culture and her subcultures. It is very challenging for a church to cross-culture reaching souls without first understanding this concept.

This is why the local church must undergo an evaluation of ministry area and its resources. A church that wishes to reach out not just to Hispanics, but to whites, Asians, and blacks all at once will probably be overwhelmed with the needs of all these groups. Yet many communities are crying out for assistance to meet the needs in these groups. A church evaluation will help understand where it can best be effective and sensitive in areas of worship styles, language, and spiritual nourishment so that it can attract and retain any visitors from the community.

The following chapter will help the average pastor in evaluating the strengths and weaknesses of the church. Evaluating the church's membership strengths and weaknesses gives the church a bird's eye view of what the church has and what it needs to bring it up to speed. It allows the pastor to handle the strategy of implementing programs that will educate the membership of the church in areas in which they are weak.

READER'S NOTES

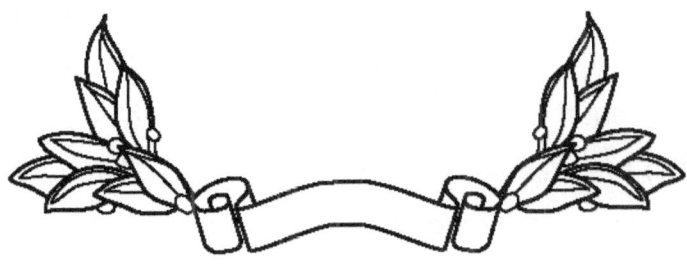

CHAPTER THREE
STRENGTHS AND WEAKNESSES
EVALUATING THE LOCAL CHURCH AND ITS LEADERS

If the readers of this book find themselves in a predicament explained in the second chapter, then a possible solution for them is to consider chapters three and four. These two chapters will help the local church leaders evaluate their strengths and weaknesses. This, in turn, will help them assess what they have available to reach the lost.

This chapter will concentrate on possible areas of strengths and weaknesses of the local church. In evaluating a church's strengths and weaknesses, the primary concern in evaluating should be the membership of a church. People's resources, the time that they can donate, their competence, as well as their formal training should all be taken into account. The more that the leaders of a church know and understand about their people's resources, the easier it is to assign jobs to members.

In the past five years of assessing church growth and church member evaluations, I have revealed to many Hispanic church leaders their reasons for their ineffectiveness in attracting and retaining visitors. The lack of understanding the importance in evaluating people's resources has led to misuse, and in some cases, abuse by

Leaders of their volunteers, not to mention the pain and hurt caused to their families.

Another area that is seldom acknowledged in evaluating personnel is the weaknesses, fears, and even personal problem people have. This is very important because generally leaders of churches give jobs to people they know very little about. In the time spent evaluating churches and their personnel, I have generally encountered that church leadership makes the mistake of placing people in jobs without regarding their abilities, talents, gifts. In finding that this problem was so prevalent, I decided to create a leadership seminar that would help pastors in general resolve this problem. To my surprise very few churches took full advantage of it. Many pastors ask why leaders placed in certain jobs do not do well and in some cases very little in a whole year. The answer is obvious: the leader was placed in a job in which he either had no interest or had very little understanding of what he was expected to do.

Fears, personal problems, and know-how have a lot to do with whether or not the leaders take the initiative. Fears have a tendency to cause a worker to rethink taking risks. Nothing is more damaging to a worker than the fear of failing and being reprimanded. When a leader begins to second guess himself he loses the ability to make good and quick decisions.

Personal problems, on the other hand, rob time, energy, and credibility from the leader or worker. They rob time in the sense that if his personal problem is weighing heavily on his mind, he will dwell more on it than on his job. The problem steals energy by occupying his emotions with worries, thus lessening the creative process. Ultimately, when a person's time, energy, and creative ability is toiled with, his credibility is compromised with his followers or superiors.

Churches which have had excellent success in using their people have discovered that placing people to work in areas where they feel competent experience much deserved success for their labors due to the fact that workers are now working from their strengths as opposed to their weaknesses. Contrarily, people who are placed in an environment where they have to consistently work from their weaknesses experience tremendous feelings of disappointment, discouragement, lack of fulfillment, and in some cases anger, rage, and ultimately failure. Having success in any part of ministry uplifts, excites, empowers, and revitalizes the ministry. Hispanic churches in particular need to spend time and resources to help the workers and leaders receive much need training and equipping. There are many Spanish courses available today in many areas that the Hispanic pastors can utilize in their churches.

RESOURCES FOR EVALUATIONS

Pastors and leaders in charge of training programs should consider establishing a department of human resources to help the evaluation process. There are many excellent instruments evaluation that can help the leaders of a church get the most from their few personnel.

Today there is an array of strategies from various resources to assist in organizing a complete program of training leaders from beginners with little experience to seasoned veterans. Churches must, for the sake of their limited personnel, take full advantage of such helps. The terminology for some of these evaluating resources varies, but most are called instruments.

One such instrument that I have used extensively in evaluating a leader is called the Personal Profile System, better known by its nickname 'Disc'. The Personal Profile System is an instrument (not a battery test) which allows pastors, leaders, and workers being evaluated to learn about their style of leadership as perceived by others, especially their followers. The Personal Profile is published by Carlson Learning Company from Minnesota and has been in use for a few decades.

It is written in many languages and is very simple to use, yet very reliable. The Disc is used to find the predominant leadership style of a person.

What makes this evaluational instrument unique is that the Disc has been prepared and tested by professionals in the respected field of behavioral psychology. The Personal Profile System has also been examined by other firms which test evaluating and testing instruments. Far above all these, the sheer numbers of Discs being used and the success by those using them gives ample proof of its worth.

The central value of the Personal Profile System is its ability to help the user better understand how other people view his leadership. In the many times that I evaluated men and women with this instrument, the comments made by the people being evaluated were of satisfaction and/or astonishment of what they learned about themselves.

Another reason for using the Carlson Learning Company in evaluating personnel is that this company makes not only the Disc instrument, but they also have an entire catalog of evaluating tools for a number of areas in need of measuring, qualifying and exploring people's potentials.

The Organizational Design and Development, Inc. is another company that produces tools for evaluating and training workers. This company also has a catalog full of seminars, apparatus, games, and projects to help churches in further developing people.

Another very important and even biblical instrument that should be taken into consideration in assessing personnel is a spiritual gifts inventory which can be bought in almost any Bible store. This tool can help enormously in assessing the spiritual gifts of church workers. It can be combined with related Scripture found in the epistles to the Romans, Corinthians, Colossians, and Ephesians.

REASONS FOR EVALUATING WORKERS

Charles Swindoll, the previous pastor of the Evangelical Free church in Fullerton, California, gave a message at Biola University when I was attending school there. From that message I have gleamed this one important message. He said, "If a company is not producing the right product or materials it is trying to sell, and its profits are falling, the company does not fire the people at the assembly lines. No, it fires the president of the company." So it is with the church. If a church is not attracting visitors for potential members and growth, the blame should not be placed on the congregation or workers of evangelism. The responsibility lies in the vision of the pastor, the governing board of the church, or both.

Truthfully, workers in today's churches are not being trained to be people-greeters. Far less than half of the church members in general have the natural elements to be good greeters. Yet every person in the church has potential to be a decent greeter. The church must evaluate itself to see where it is missing the mark. To do very little or nothing is to limit growth potentials in the church.

The most important reason for evaluating anyone is to have a good understanding of where to place that person to utilize to the ultimate degree his abilities. As stated before, knowing where and how to utilize a person allows him or her to be a great asset; not knowing can make him or her a liability. Depending on the outcome of such an individual's performance, the church is either going to benefit or fall farther behind.

Pastors and leaders who have difficulty in understanding the development of workers and the jobs assigned to them create workers every year who rarely succeed. Most congregations only have a certain number of workers and leaders. If they are not used carefully, the church may find

Itself with members having a low morale.

Workers who have not been used correctly find that after a while they do not want to help in church business affairs. They stay away from leading and assist only in those projects that will not further aggravate them. What happens to churches of this nature is that the pastor and a few workers end up doing all the work. Eventually, even those workers get burned out. When I was doing consultative work among the Hispanic churches, I developed a slogan to shock the church leaders. It read, "The greatest obstacle in any leadership is the leader's lack of understanding to lead." The church's leaders must learn what great obstacles they face in growing their church. In most cases those great obstacles are usually caused by the leadership itself.

As a church evaluates its progress, it is going to find itself in one of three areas of growth. The first area of growth concern (and these areas are not necessarily in order) is when the church is growing sufficiently to keep it moving forward. It is attracting and retaining enough visitors to show that what they are doing is good enough. Probably more should be done, but for right now, they are doing all right. The church has programs and activities that are currently visitor friendly. This type of church is in a good position to continue attracting the unchurched and has potential for increasing quality programs that can contribute to great numbers of growth.

The second area of growth concern is when the church is not growing nor is it declining in membership. It is not sustaining any loses, but it is not increasing its size. The church knows that it is attracting and retaining very little visitors. They are concerned with the few visitors they are attracting, but they are having trouble identifying what should be done to remedy the situation. This church does not understand how they are attracting or what visitors are coming to their church. This is not a complicated problem to resolve. More will be said later about the solutions needed for this case.

The third area of growth concern is when the church is not attracting visitors at all, and is even losing current members. The concern of the leadership is at an all time high, and the low morale is affecting the church. The church at this stage is probably having a great turnover in pastors, leaders, and members. Low morale in both leadership and membership robs the church of its blessings and joy. The personnel that could have been able to turn around this situation is probably gone. There are most likely no youth or young married couples in this body of believers. Only the long standing diehards and the pioneers of this congregation keeping it going. It is very difficult to attract visitors at this level, but not impossible. A great number of churches are in this third type of predicament and do not even know or care. At this point, it must be defined what low morale looks like and does to a congregation and its leadership. Many leaders are confused as to what low morale looks like and the impact it can have on them.

Defining Low Morale

The first area of concern of course is the spiritual side of the people. If the spirit of the people is low, something must be done to bring it up. Bringing up people's spirits is not always an easy to accomplish. In fact, the worst symptom of a beaten church is low morale.

Low morale relates to the self esteem of the people. In other words, it is how people feel toward something they love or care a great deal about. If leaders and members do not feel anything for their church to invest time, effort, and financial resources, the condition of that church will not change. If the feelings of the people cannot be turned around so they feel good about themselves, they will not be so inclined to invest anything of themselves. Fear of failure again has deep roots. If the congregation still sees the possibility of failure, then the chances of investing are nullified.

If low morale is present in any congregation, then the first response by the leader is to discover what caused the low morale. It is a well-known sports strategy that the best defense is a great offense. In order for a leader to help his church out of a terrible morale problem, he must know the cause.

A sure way that can help a church lift its spirit again, at least temporarily, is to see itself doing what it was called to do. I have never seen a church not get excited when someone comes to tho Lord. Even Scripture says that when a convert comes to salvation, there is rejoicing in heaven by the angels.[1] How much more of a rejoicing should a church of believers have?

Believers with low morale should not be expected to begin immediate soul reaching efforts. Just because they rejoiced for one or more souls saved does not remove their spirit out of their predicament-it merely relieves their low self esteem for a while. Their mental, physical, and spiritual circumstances must be programmed to believe that the almighty God in heaven will once again empower them and their church for ministry. Many obstacles work against the development of the believers to become ardent

---

[1] Luke 15:10, Luke's quotation of what Christ said of a sinner repenting.

soul winners. The pastor or leader must be familiar with spiritual warfare. He must be thoroughly familiar with prayer fasting and be sensitive to the guidance of the Holy Spirit.

Designing leadership to work efficiently is the most complex system of church growth known to date. Most pastors and leaders do not know the basics in designing a plan to develop leaders and workers. Many leaders and Christian workers are given ministries, jobs, and things to do with little or no job description or ministry boundaries.

Helping people overcome their low self esteem and thus lift the low morale takes time and personal attention. Depending on the severity of the self esteem, workers might have to be closely led for particular job, ministerial positions, and/or ministries.

At first, they might have to be given jobs or objectives that will help them do simple things to help raise their confidence. As the confidence increases, so will the independence of the workers increase. As stated earlier, depending on the severity of the people's spirit and faith in themselves and God, the pastor or leader might have to walk with them from the beginning in training them.

SPIRITUAL GIFTS

In the body of Christ today, there is a much needed understanding of the use of spiritual gifts. For a long time many have contended that these gifts were fulfilled and ended with the first century church. But all who read the same Scriptures do nut agree. For those who agree that they are useful and applicable today, I challenge you to begin by reading all that has been writ· ten on this topic. Read the Word of God where it speaks of the spiritual gifts. Interview pastors who are successfully implementing the use of such gifts. Remember that these gifts are for the administering of, as well as ministering to the body of Christ. Both saved and unsaved are ministered to by these gifts. These gifts of leadership empower men and women to lead their churches with great faith and dedication. The areas of Scripture where the gifts are mentioned should be examined. It is the apostle Paul who writes the most about spiritual gifts in the New Testament. The gifts given to believers are a service of love to all who receive them. The apostle Paul states this in Romans chapter 12. He encourages the Roman church in this chapter to present their "bodies as a living sacrifice, holy, acceptable unto God, which is our reasonable service."[2]

---

[2] **Epistle to the Romans 12:1 ff, Paul's exhortation of the life presented before God.**

Spiritual gifts are given to men and women for service. This service is to be administered by the saints to all who need it. The Paul proceeds to explain the various gifts given to believers. In verses 6 through 8 the apostle Paul emphasizes the following gifts:

> "Having then gifts differing according to the grace that is given to us, whether prophecy, let us prophesy according to the proportion of faith: Or ministry, let us wait on our ministering: or he that teacheth, on teaching; or he that exhorteth, on exhortation: he that giveth, let him do it with simplicity: he that ruleth, with diligence; he that showeth mercy, with cheerfulness."[3]

The apostle Paul mentions seven gifts that are given to believers: prophecy, ministry, teaching, exhortation, giving, administration, and mercy. All of these gifts are for the body of Christ and her growth. No one to whom a gift is given ought to think of himself higher in category or in anything else. Rather, the believers ought to consider themselves members of the same body, but with different offices.

Another passage which addresses spiritual gifts is found in 1 Corinthians 12. Two-thirds of the way through the writing of this epistle, the apostle Paul inserts a chapter of gifts for the believers of this area. He begins the

---

[3] Romans 12:6-8 ff, Paul's explanation of the spiritual gifts in the believer's service of love.

Chapter by telling his readers that he will not tolerate ignorance concerning the spiritual gifts.

The following is a quotation from verses 1-11:

> "Now concerning spiritual gifts, brethren, I would not have you ignorant. Ye know that ye were Gentiles, carried away unto these dumb idols, even as ye were led. Wherefore I give you to understand, that no man speaking by the Spirit of God calleth Jesus accursed and that no man can say that Jesus is the Lord, but by the Holy Ghost. Now there are diversities of gifts but the same Spirit. And there are differences of administrations, but the same Lord. And there are diversities of operations, but it is the same God which worketh all in all. But the manifestations of the Spirit is given to every man to profit withal. For to one is given by the Spirit the word of wisdom; to another the word of knowledge by the same Spirit; To another faith by the same Spirit; to another prophecy; to another discerning of spirits; to another divers kinds of tongues; to another the interpretation of tongues: But all these worketh that one and the selfsame Spirit, dividing to every man severally as he will."4

The apostle Paul continues to elaborate on the body and its members concept that he began in Romans 12. In 1 Corinthians 12, the apostle Paul develops the body metaphor more fully. It is interesting how he discusses his own gifts in 2 Corinthian 10 as he shares his own spiritual authority. In verse 13 he writes" according to the measure

---

4 1 Corinthians 12:1 ff, Paul's explanation of the spiritual gifts and their responsibility to the believer

of the rule which God has distributed to us, a measure to reach even unto people." It seems as if this "measure to reach" is an extent of the preaching gift given to him. Note verse 16 where he exhorts them "to preach the Gospel in the regions beyond them, and not to boast in an another man's line of things made ready to our hand."

The concept of one planting and another watering was part of the body metaphor. We are encourage by the apostle Paul to act like the members of , our body in working for God.

The apostle also made another very interesting comment in verse 14, where he writes, "For we stretch not ourselves beyond our measure, as though we reach not unto you: for we are come as far as to you also in preaching the Gospel of Christ." It seems as though some gifts may have limitations by the Spirit of God in the way that the Spirit measured out the gift. It sounds as if the limitation has to do with the extent to which the Holy Spirit desires to take it.

Why is this information about the gifts important to tho recruitment of visitors? In Luke chapter 10, Jesus sends forth the 70 to the surrounding towns and villages to take the Gospel of the kingdom of God. He gives them instructions as to what He wants them to do and say:

Luke 10:1-6:

> "Therefore said he unto them, The harvest truly is great but the laborers are few: pray ye therefore the Lord of the harvest, that he would send forth laborers into his harvest. Go your ways: behold, I send you forth as lambs among wolves. Carry neither purse, nor scrip, nor shoes: and salute no man by the way. And into whatsoever house ye enter, first say Peace be to this house. And if the son [head of the household] of peace be there, your peace shall rest upon it: if not, it shall turn to you again.[5]

If the church follows the example that Christ left with this passage, it is to send its 70--those disciples trained to do the work of God-into the harvest. In the field of attracting visitors or visiting unchurched people, the church is to train its members to use what God has given them for the work of the ministry. In this case, what God has given them are the spiritual gifts. If the believers do not know what the Holy Spirit has given them and do not know how to use it, the yield of their labors may be very small. Believers must be taught that everything the Scripture teach belongs to them for their own good use. This was what the New Testament church understood and what helped in their success.

---

[5] Luke 10:1-6, Luke's explanation of what Christ told Seventy Disciples.

Believers too must look into everything that the Bibles teaches and lean how to use it to be successful in reaching this generation. Leaders learn to work with people or programs more effectively if they understand their calling, office, and gifts. In the epistle to the Ephesians chapter 4 and verses 11-16, the apostle Paul gives another summary:

> And he gave some, apostles; and some, prophets; and some, evangelists; and some, pastors and teachers; for the perfecting of the saints, for the work of the ministry, for the edifying of the body of Christ: Till we all come in the unity of the faith, and of the knowledge of the Son of God, unto a mature man, reaching the measure of the stature of the fullness of Christ:6

This portion of Scripture further demonstrates the development of the offices, calling, and gifts of which the apostle Paul has been developing with the help of the Holy Spirit for these vocations are revealed according to verse 12, these gifts are given for 3 reasons. The first is for the equipping of the saints In these portion of Scripture, the reasons for these vocations are revealed. According to verse 12, these gifts are given for 3 reasons. The first is for the equipping of the saints, the second is for the work of the ministry, and the third is for the building up of the saints. This is to be continued until the body of

---

6 Ephesians 4:1-13, Paul's explanation of the unity of the Spirit.

Christ becomes unified in faith, grown in the knowledge of the Son of God, a mature man, unto the measure of the stature the fullness of Christ.

The last part of this passage gives a more detailed explanation of what Paul wrote in 1 Corinthians 12:28:

> "And God hath some in the church, first apostles, secondarily prophets, thirdly hers, after that miracles, then gifts of healings, helps, governments, different kinds of tongues."

Some have separated the three as offices. However, the other gifts are in the same context. If the first three are offices, then the last five are offices too. Scripture must be interpreted consistently.

There are other portions of Scripture where the gifts are mention. In Acts 6:3, the request of the apostles for men of honest full of the Holy Ghost and wisdom shows prudence of Wisdom has already been seen in other lists, but what of the term *"full of the Holy Ghost?"* Could this be a gift? In Acts 2:38, the apostle Peter is telling the people how they are to be baptized.

> "Then Peter said unto them, Repent, and be baptized every one of you in the name of Jesus Christ for the remission of your sins, and you shall receive the gift of the Holy Spirit."[7]

---

[7] 1 Peter 4:10, Peter's admonishment of ministering one to another.

In the English language, the word for gift is simple to understand. In the greek language, the word used for gift has several connotations. Some of the gifts are gifts of grace on the part of God as a donor. Others are free gifts stressing His gratuitous character, or act of giving. They are all gifts to be used in the service of God.

It was not only the apostle Paul who wrote about the gifts. The apostle Peter also mentioned the use of these gifts by good stewards of God's grace. In 1 Peter 4:10, he speaks about using the gifts which God has given to minister one to another. "As every man hath received the gift, even so minister the same one to another, as good stewards of the manifold grace of God.[7]

The pastor who is able to understand how to use gifts of his congregation knows better where to place his members to reach maximum usage of those gifts. The spiritual gifts given to individuals are a sure sign from God regarding His desires in growing His church. This was the reason that the first century church was so successful. They learned the movement of the Holy Spirit through the believer's spiritual gifts.

The pastor who desires his congregation to grow is the pastor who understands that he cannot do all the work of growing that body of believers alone. He must become the head that directs the body. He must learn how to unleash the hidden energy in his people. He must learn how to tap into what God give His children.

Through the understanding of the believer's gift in, a pastor may be able to draw a clear and complete picture of where the Holy Spirit wishes to direct His church. Many times believer's gifts may cluster within a certain category of healing, evangelizing, teaching, or reconciliation, allowing the pastor to discover where and with whom to begin ministry. At other times, the believer's gifts may be spread quite evenly throughout the range of all the gifts. Whatever the case, the pastor should examine the vision or direction that the Holy Spirit is signaling.

In my ventures of consulting Hispanic churches, I have come to value men and women visionaries who create with a potent force a special climate which enables the church's values and vision to energize, pervade, and direct every ministry, activity, and operation. The potent force that enables values and vision to be applied is the same force that unleashes the creative power of people and breathes new life into the church's work.

That potent force is the guidance of the Holy Spirit.

While vision helps dream dreams, direction helps steer the dreams toward fulfillment. Some people call direction the mission or objective. The reason for using the term direction instead of mission or objectives is that it is very difficult to conceive a dream and make it work successfully at first without having something go wrong. No idea or dream can grow legs and start running. It must be allowed to crawl and walk for a while, Just as a large ship needs tugboats to direct it out of port unto the open sea, so does a dream need direction to set it in the right course. Once the direction has firmly been given, then the dream or vision can be guided to help it move.

Godly Vision and Direction

Another evaluation that the local church must do concerning its calling as a body of believers is to come to an under standing of the vision and direction that the Holy Spirit is leading or trying to give. Godly vision and direction comes from God. There is no way that a natural man can come up with godly values and direction on his own. If a man wants to serve his creator in the capacity of a servant leading people to the kingdom of God, he must first go to his Master and search out Go's plan for his life and for the church for which he is responsible.

God gave men natural talents to earn a living and be responsible to the created order and their families. He also gave all believers spiritual gifts to use in the government and growth of the church. Spiritual gifts are one of the areas that have been given very little attention. When a pastor and church leaders learn to use wisely the spiritual gifts that God has given them, they will learn the plan of God. As mentioned before, utilizing the believer's spiritual gift inventory can help a great deal in learning which believer has been given what spiritual gift to use in the church's growth.

Godly Leadership

What is godly leadership? Godly leadership is the capacity to lead others with divine character, attributes, and personality. It is far more an attitude than anything else. Reaching the lost and troubled souls requires godly leadership. Attracting souls will demand that those reaching out to them be genuine sons and daughters of the living God.

Ted W. Engstrom in his book <u>The Making of a Christian Leader</u> states this about the people who are being reached:

> "Our nation and world today are faced with problems that appear insurmountable. Security and defense problems are staggering. For the most part, our youth

our future leaders, are confused, alienated, and demoralized. Morals are at an all-time low. Moral standards are almost nonexistent. The growing national debt, bankrupt nations, financially troubled cities, and economic instability create more alarm each passing day. Amid these grave circumstances, our generation is facing an equally serious problem: a leadership crisis." 8

Ted Engstrom wrote this book in the mid-70's. He never imagined what this nation would look like in the mid-90's. The national debt is in the trillions. It is said that today's children will have to pay two-thirds of their paycheck to the government to repay the debt that their parents left.

In the same book, Ted W. Engstrom states the following about leadership:

"Though leadership may be hard to define, the one characteristic common to all leaders is the ability to make things happen-to act in order to help others work in an environment within which each individual serving under him finds himself encouraged and stimulated to a point where he is helped to realize his fullest potential to contribute meaningfully." 9

As stated earlier, leadership has more to do with the attitude of the leader than his actions. His actions and possible consequences are dictated by his attitude.

---

8 Ted W. Engstrom, The Making of a Leader (Grand Rapids, MI: Zondervan Publishing House, 1976), pg. 12.

9 Ted W. Engstrom, pg. 12.

Because leadership an attitude, one can be a lord over his followers, or one can be a servant to motivate people to follow. David L. Mckenna seems to agree with this in his book <u>Power to Follow, Grace to Lead</u> when he writes:

> "Secular leadership theory tends to emphasize the organization and the process more than the person. When secular theory does emphasize the person, the attributes of competence and charisma tend to be more important than character. A secular leader may be born with natural abilities and taught certain skills which enhance leadership quality, but the resources for leadership are limited to human dimensions. Christian leadership is different be cause it centers in the character of the person and engages spiritual as well as human resources."[10]

Godly leadership must be evaluated from the standpoint of godly motives. Leadership that is biblical seeks to lead with a style that is servant oriented. The attitude should be to serve and build up others as opposed to self. The leadership that desires to lord over its followers merely lusts after self praise, benefit, and prestige. This type of leadership is anti-biblical. Matthew relates the following discourse between Jesus and one ambitious mother:

---

[10] David L. McKenna, <u>Power to Follow, Grace to Lead</u> (Dallas, TX: Word Publishing House, 1989), pg. 29.

"Then came to him the mother of Zebedee's children with her sons, worshipping him, and desiring a certain thing of him. And he said unto her, What wilt thou? She saith unto him, Grant that these my two sons may sit, the one on thy right hand, and the other on the left, in they kingdom. But Jesus answered and said, Ye know not what ye ask. Are ye able to drink of the cup that I shall drink of, and to be baptized with the baptism that I am baptized with? They say unto him, We are able. And he saith unto) them, Ye shall drink indeed of my cup, and be baptized with tho baptism that I am baptized with: but to sit on my right hand, and on my left, is not mine to give, but it shall be given to them fur whom it is prepared of my Father. And when the ten heard it, they were moved with indignation against the two brethren. But Jesus called them unto) him, and said, ye know that the princesses of the Gentiles exercise dominion over them, and they that are great exercise authority upon them. But it shall not be so among you: but whosoever will be great among you, let him be your minister; And whosoever will be chief among you, let him be your servant: Even as the Son of man came not to be ministered unto, but to minister, and to give his life a ransom for many."[11]

Jesus Christ, the Son of God, had more reasons to lord his authority over people than anyone else in His creation. Instead, He chose to demonstrate the heart of a true leader by his attitude and actions as Jesus the servant according to Mark's gospel. Godly leaders influence from within by encouraging, spiring, and motivating.

---

[11] Matthew 20:20-28, Christ's admonishment of servant leadership.

They enjoy developing good relationships with their co-workers, thus helping them to grow. Frank Damazio in his book The Making: of a Leader correctly differentiates between godly motives and secular motives. He states:

> "In surveying the characteristics of a godly leader, we cannot avoid seeing that pure and spiritual motives in the heart give rise to growth. By contrast, if a leader seeks high position sheerly for exaltation, he will only use people to his own ends, rather than serving their needs. Further more, if a leader wants primarily to make people dependent upon his presence (thus giving him a sense of power), he will never properly train those under him who desire to be used of the Lord. God sets tremendous importance on a leader's reasons and motives. The wrong motives will poison a leader's work, while the right motives will overcome a host of difficulties."[12]

In explaining godly motives, Frank Damazio clearly illustrates the qualities of the godly leader. He states the following:

> "On the other hand, the motivations that God wants to see in the lives of His leaders are the motivations that will impel us upward. A desire to serve others and meet the needs, to make them successful in their calling and ministries, as Jonathan did for David. A hunger to show the love and mercy of God to those that so desperately need it. A deep, stubborn commitment to be faithful to the will of God in our lives. An urgency to lead others to Christ. A need to unite family members under Christ's headship. A drive to help the spiritually sick, poor and oppressed."[13]

---

[12] Frank Damazio, The Making of a Leader (Portland OR, Bible Temple Publishing, 1988), pg. 32.

[13] Damazio, pg. 33.

The two quotes of Frank Damazio help explain the importance of godly leadership to properly exercise the abilities of the church members and workers to attract and retain visitors. Nothing else can motivate members of a church to be more all aggressive and sensitive to unchurched visitors for retention. The example set by the church leaders in visitor friendliness must be very transparent and contagious so that it automatically motivates the members to effectively interact with new visitors.

READER'S NOTES

ACTION STEPS

1. A self-evaluation questionnaire must be completed on all areas and departments of the church. George Barna of Barna research produces a self administered, user friendly inventory that is excellent for evaluating thirteen areas in the church. [14]

2. A self-evaluation survey on the sensitivity of visitors should be performed. HRDQ, a company that produces learning resources for maximizing individual and teams, produces a training course which has a built-in survey that teaches people to put the customers in first place. It can easily be adapted to fit the church. [15]

3. Complete a self-evaluation survey on the leadership church to examine the goals, priorities, and philosophy of ministry the church has and desires to continue to use. The comprehensive leader course that HRDQ puts out can be very effective in this area. [16]

---

[14] George Barna, The User Friendly Inventory, Glendale, CA, 1992.

[15] HRD Quarterly, Organization Design and Development, Inc., (King of Prussia, PA, 1997), pg. 41.

[16] HRD Quarterly, pg. 16.

4. Conduct a self-evaluation survey on the community in which the church has been working to see if the church still has viable resources to reach the community. Unfortunately, there are not many resources available to examine or survey a community for what the church needs. The church can produce a questionnaire of its own. The questions should be taken from what the church is searching for in the visitors it wishes to attract.

SUMMARY

The importance of this chapter in assessing the church's resources is paramount to the work ahead of it. To be able to understand what the church has in its arsenal of resources and what the Holy Spirit desires to do with it is vital. Though the true God-sent pastor might have a very good idea of what the Lord wishes to do with that church, knowing what resources are available for the church to use in reaching the lost is another thing. There is no excuse for making bad decisions these days. There is a lot help for the pastor that wants to get ahead of the competition. In the following chapter, there will be information covering some ideas and techniques in doing a community assessment. This is not a comprehensive chapter, but there are ideas concerning how to learn more about the community one wishes to reach.

READER'S NOTES

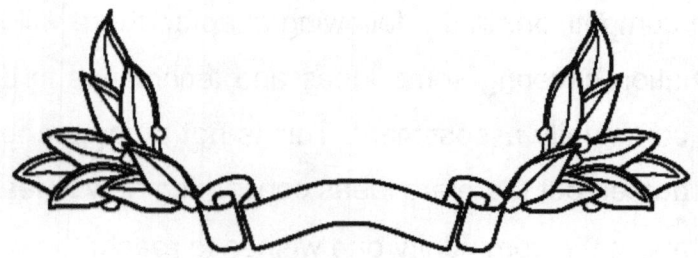

CHAPTER FOUR
COMMUNITY EVALUATION
*A*SSESSING *C*OMMUNITY *N*EEDS

Assessing community needs is the flip side of training church leadership. There must be a good reason to embark on organizing and training members and leaders of a church. The principle reason should be to find, attract, and retain visitors for the growth of the church. Yet where does the church go to find these visitors? What communities, neighborhoods, cities, and parks will be visited to search for souls? The church, in general, has tried some or all of the common challenges known to the average congregation. It has either gone door to door witnessing, encouraged members to bring visitors, or has waited for visitors to walk in off the street.

In chapter two, examples were given about three kinds of churches. One was growing with a reasonable number of visitors every Sunday from whom they could draw future members. Another was growing enough to maintain the number the church likes to have. The last was losing members and was decreasing rapidly.

A church in a community which has a large number of type W people (white, middle to upper income) and very low numbers of type B (black), H (Hispanic), and A (Asians) cultures, will have a sufficient number of Type W members from which to evangelize. If, however, the situation is reversed and the predominant number of people of that community are type B, H, and A cultures, then the church with the type W members will have a very small number of W visitors to draw into the church's programs and activities. In this case, it does not matter how large ministry area the church has. If the kind of people they want to draw into their fold is very small, then they will experience little growth. Because time waits for no one, it stands to reason that the church that clings to one kind of group of people may wake up one day to find that the largest segment of people they like to draw from have moved away and the people that now occupy their ministry area are strangers to them.

Churches that remain in communities with their original profile of people, worship style, and programs while the community is undergoing a cultural change might find themselves in a fortress mentality. What makes a difference between a successful church and one that is merely maintaining is the number of souls reachable in the surrounding community. If the number of souls a church hopes to reach is unavailable for whatever reason, the church will not grow. Sometimes what keeps a church a live for quite a long time is the people commuting to the church from outside the community.

CULTURE CHANGING COMMUNITIES

If one culture leaves and another comes into a community, there is usually a long transitional period. These community turnovers do not just happen overnight. Businesses, schools, city governments, and churches have plenty of time to adapt to and change. Any business that serves the community but resists the change that is happening in its area is bound to suffer financial losses, possibly even bankruptcy. In the case of the church that refuses to change with the needs of the community, the body of believers of the church will not interact. In some cases, the church may repel the incoming culture, causing friction and alienation between them. These congregations take great steps in preserving themselves. Some of these steps can include building walls or fences around the churches' properties to protect themselves from the new arrivals. Other steps include buying additional buildings to support all that their members can possibly need within their fortress, everything from sports facilities to dinning halls.

Frank R. Tillapaugh in his book Unleashing the Church gives an excellent definition of what the fortress church looks like.

He writes:
> The Fortress church put up its building, starts its programs and concentrates primarily within its walls. The church unleashed is not unconcerned with what goes on within its church buildings, but it is only partial focused there. In the church unleashed an individual's primary ministry may be within one of many traditional church programs such as Sunday school.[1]

In his second book Unleashing Your Potential Tillapaugh again gives his version of what he means by the term "fortress mentality." He writes:
> "In a few words, the fortress mentality says the church will minister to anyone who will come within the four walls of our church buildings, and fit in with us."[2]

The fortress mentality is, unfortunately, predominant in too many churches. It is this mentality that can very easily cripple people and stop them from going into their neighborhoods and ministry areas to make an impact. This mentality hinders people in all ways because it requires that all programs and activities be done within the four walls of their church. It is like comparing how many fish will be caught in a pond using a fly-fishing pole verses a net in an ocean. The fortress mentality limits people's fishing ability by confining them to fish for sport instead

---

[1] Frank Tillapaugh, Unleashing Your Potential, (Ventura, CA: Regal books, 1982), pg. 8.

[2] Tillapaugh, pgs. 22-23.

of fishing commercially. Sport fishing is for pleasure and relaxation. It is for fun and for collecting trophies and awards. In contrast, commercial fishing is for an occupation; it is for living. The apostle Matthew in his Gospel writes of Christ's view in this matter. He states:

> "And Jesus, walking by the sea of Galilee, saw two brethren, Simon called Peter, and Andrew his brother, casting a net into the sea: for they were fisherman. And he saith unto them, Follow me, and I will make you fishers of men. And they straightway left their nets, and followed him."[3]

Culture changing communities mostly affect the churches that are of the third type. This church, which will eventually have fewer and fewer visitors and members supporting its congregation, will no doubt feel the greatest pressure to survive in its facilities. The same pioneers and diehards who continue in the church are probably the same ones who refused to leave with the original members, and who resist any incoming community members. What will happen to the children of the pioneers and diehards? The children of these pioneers who decide to stay with their parents in the culture changing communities will have to learn to interact and interrelate with the incoming culture.

---

[3] Matthew 4:18-20, Christ's selection of His disciples.

The intermarriage and offspring of these children will begin the process of a new subgroup or subculture spoken of earlier. Depending on the strict values of the incoming culture or the inflexibility of the current membership, the church will either change and grow or eventually die. Furthermore, the intermarriage of such children can cause tremendous pressures within the families. There will tend to be some proselytizing from both cultures in regard to values, beliefs, traditions and even church affiliation. Though the parents of the mixed marriages desire proselytizing to work, the church members will not be so sympathetic.

In America today, subcultures are a mix or blend of values between two cultures that intermarry. Identification with their own values and culture is still relatively strong. It is not until the birth of the offspring in the intermarriage that identity with one culture or the other begins to be lost. This offspring then becomes a subculture. An identity crisis forms in the first generation.

Many first generation children often reject the mother culture or motherland. As these children hear their parents talk about the "good old country" and how it used to be, they cannot identify with it as their heritage. The world where they are growing up gives them all that they need to assimilate. In fact, when the children are taken to the old country, many of them begin to reject it and all it stands for. As they grow older, the rejection increases to the point that when the parents visit their families, the children do not go with them. Many parents at this stage cannot understand why their children do not want to go, but eventually accept it.

When I was doing a class-church related internship during my days at Talbot School of Theology, I internship with a church by the name of Church on Brady." The pastor was and still is Tom Wolve. He had written a book entitled "Oikos Evangelism." That church had gone through a culture-community change. Originally, I believe, it was a Baptist church/congregation. He had been brought in to pastor and when he became familiar with the problems of growth in that church, his suggestions to the remaining congregation were to shift their attraction to the Hispanics that were in their ministry area. The term '**ministry area**' is defined as, "a reasonable driving distance from the church, usually 15-25 minutes." 4

---

4 Win Arn, The Church Growth Ration Book (Pasadena, CA: Church Growth, Inc,. 1997), 47.

The people that lived in their ministry area were both black and Hispanic with some lingering white people. It was on this account that he wrote the book <u>Oikos Evangelism</u>. I remember my professor of church growth, Dr. Harold Dollar, that the Church on Brady could attract first and even second generational Hispanics, but not the traditional or the Third generation. At first, I did not comprehend what they were talking about, but today I have a much better understanding of this phenomenon. This problem will be explained in the fifth chapter. The Church on Brady is a good example of one culture leaving and another one taking its place.

As one culture leaves, a new one arrives, and in time another may come in to repeat the cycle all over again. Only this time the subculture does not have strong values and traditions give its adherents anchors to hold on to in the change. What happens in such a turnover is that the second incoming culture takes over much more quickly than the previous one. This merger produces territorial disputes. The end result in all this is the birth of subculture terrorists, better known today as gangs.

One might ask, "Where is the community church while all this is happening?" The answer is very obvious. The

Local church has alienated itself from all that is happening in the community. The church has closed its doors and retreated within its walls.

Another may ask, "But are not there any other churches reaching these people?" The answer again is obvious. Unless a church from that area becomes interested, there will be nobody reaching these people. A church from the community of which the incoming culture comes might decide to plant a mission in this new area. However that will only happen if the incoming culture is Christianized. The chances of this happening are slim.

In assessing a community, one must also take into account several areas of concern such as: areas under develop, projects, apartment sections, bedroom communities, industrial cites, commercial and business areas, and even freeways.

Size of the Community

The first step is to determine the size of the ministry area the church will reach in the community. The size of the community area includes the geographical area in terms of housing development and the people living there. Why does the size of the community have any bearing on assessing it? The answer will become apparent to any

church if it answers the following questions:
1. First, is the community growing, stabilizing, or shrinking?
2. Second, why is the community growing, stabilizing, or shrinking?
3. Third, who is causing the growing, stabilizing, or shrinking?
4. Fourth, where is most of this growing or shrinking happening?
5. Fifth, who or what is being affected by the growing or shrinking?

In ascertaining the reason for growth of any community one will find that people with similar needs have a tendency to flock together. For example, if an area in an older community is heavily concentrated with industrial or commercial jobs, but the housing industry is down, overly priced, or saturated, the workers of such an area will seek the nearest place to find housing, even if they have to drive several hours. A scenario of this sort has caused areas previously dormant to become bedroom communities. The growth of housing superseded the community's master plan of growth. Thus, practically over night a rural community can come alive with people flocking to buy new houses.

This in turn causes that community to begin building schools, shopping centers, hospitals, streets, day care centers, and all that goes with a growing community.

What if a community is not growing, but is stabilized? The church performing the assessment should find out if the community has areas free for growth. Can the community furnish current and future plans of its vision of tomorrow? Is there any room for growth? How old is the community? Are businesses, industries or people moving away from the area? The answers for all of these questions may give evidence of a conclusive stable community.

Normally, a shrinking community can be viewed in terms of the number of people, businesses or industries moving away. A community that is not attracting, but losing industries and businesses can be labeled as a community that is shrinking. The idea of shrinkage can even be used to describe the number of jobs, businesses, and industries needed to maintain the population in that community from leaving. In the same context, a shrinking community can refer to a homogeneous group of people in a community whose number is rapidly decreasing. Sometimes shrinkage is less noticeable because of industries leaving an area ever so slowly. By the time a community becomes aware of it, it is probably too late to do anything about it.

An example of this would be the communities that sprang up around cities that built cars for a living. When the automobile industry went under so did all associated businesses and light industries. Other areas that provided raw material such as steel, glass, plastic, etc. also suffered economic depression. People had for a long time been feeling the pinch in one way or another, but were probably hoping it would turn around.

All of the above research and answers can paint a more accurate picture of the community that is being targeted. The better the quality of research the church does, the easier the search for souls. No amount of research can be too much. Denominations that can afford this type of research for their local churches will find the trend and flow of souls for their local churches to grow. In fact, when new communities are on the rise and people are moving in to settle them, denominations should be tracking such pathways of people-movements so as to plant churches in those new communities.

The second area of research will answer the assessor's question as to where to deploy the church's resources and man power. As stated before, the bulk of small churches do not have resources and manpower to do what the larger or mega churches can do. Thus, a well planned strategy in the assessment of a community can reap many benefits. Unfortunately, many churches choose to be located in the areas in which they are currently ministering for the wrong reasons. When a body of believers is growing, the pastor usually with a committee begin looking for a better, bigger place to meet for worship. Often the reason for finding a place is not because they have found an area that is ripe with souls, hungry for the Gospel but, instead, the reasons are generally and primarily based on money. New or larger building search committees have a tendency to research and target buildings based on the type of building they are looking for and can afford, instead of targeting a building where their visitors will most likely be found. There are other options that could be looked into, but generally search committees want a building that looks like a church, even if the building houses about one-third the seating capacity needed to pay for the purchase of it.

The third question of research can answer a variety of much needed information about who to reach. It can answer questions like what will the profile of the church look like if a certain area or people group is targeted? Will the church need to change its current profile? If so, how much will it have to change? How soon and how fast will this change overtake the church? And tho most important question:, can this church handle the change?

The **who** question can answer the **where to go** dilemma as well as answering **how many** different kinds of people live within this community. It can also help with the answer to **what will attract them.** The reason why unchurched people are flocking or staying in that area of the community will answer what the church is needing to do.

All of these answers can help the church's strategy in designing what will attract visitors from those places. The culture being evangelized can help explain such things in reaching them by understanding the kind of Christian music they will most likely enjoy, the style of worship they will desire, the language they most likely communicate effectively in, and the level of education that it will take to transmit the Gospel to them.

The reason for assessing in this way is because the church needs to comprehend the level of need and reach ability that the unchurched find themselves in. Besides understanding where these people are, the leaders of the church must also learn the needs of the community that might house the future members of their church.

This knowledge is extremely important if the church wishes to come into contact with this community.

Understanding the culture and its demands will aid many churches in reaching more effectively those who are lost in it. Christ very pointedly expressed this in His ministry when He fed multitudes before preaching to them. At the wedding of Cana, Christ demonstrated the importance of special festivities in the Jewish culture. Christ's journeys to the temple allowed Him to preach to the masses because He knew they would be there also.

BOUNDARIES IN THE COMMUNITY

Other areas of concern in understanding the profile of communities are natural and man-made boundaries. Natural boundaries include rivers, hills, lakes, ponds and mountains. Many of these boundaries tend to partition the community into various parts. These types of natural boundaries have a tendency to curve the growth of communities. Certain boundaries attract particular elements which need them for their use. For example, a river is used by factories, manufacturing plants, transportation agencies, and agricultural fields for their use in producing a product or providing some sort of activity or service. Lakes, for instance, have a way of attracting recreational activities.

Sports such as: fishing, boating, water skiing, swimming, and other related activities are associated with lakes. Natural boundaries do help a community to parcel itself early in its development.

Unlike natural boundaries, man-made boundaries are created by the city planners for the use of its citizens.. Man-made boundaries can be domains such as city parks, water canals, residential areas, commercial and industrial zoning, freeways, streets, railroad tracks, businesses and shopping malls, light and heavy factories, and the like. These man-made boundaries are usually build for the use of all citizens of the community. In time they can cause separation of the community's various economic levels. Parts of the city will undoubtedly require and build expensive homes, other parts will build housing for middle class, and still other parts of the community will be given for low housing projects.

As the community goes through its cultural changes, these man-made boundaries tend to become territorial markings for subcultures. These boundaries then mark alienable areas for the subgroups, distinguishing themselves from other areas in the same community. Where once these boundaries were used to fence whole parts of the city for the protection of its citizens, They now be come walls of separations, alienating one subgroup from another because of hatred or mistrust of the other.

To better illustrate how essential boundaries are, note the study done by the Western Economic Research Co., Inc. of the Hispanic growth over a period of five decades in the five county areas of Los Angeles.5 A map was taken of the five county area of Los Angeles. Using transparency overlays, the decade census population of Hispanics in all areas of growth were filled in. Through these overlays one can see just how much Hispanics are growing and where they are concentrating each decade. This reveals their priorities in their lives in each decade. This project proved to be very effective in showing Just where Hispanics concentrated themselves.

Beginning with the paper drawing of the five country area man-made boundaries tend to become territorial markings for subcultures. These boundaries then mark alienable areas for the subgroups, distinguishing themselves from other areas in the same community. Where once these bouncaries were used to fence whole parts of the city for the protection and services, today they are used more by drug dealers, gangs, and other sub-culture needs.

---

5 Western Economic Research Co., Inc., **Hispanic Los Angeles 1950- 1990** (Los Angeles,CA: Census Tract Count.

The 1960's Census chart shows the new concentrations. In the north by interstate 5, there is a second concentration in the city of Pacoima. This concentration is separated by highway 118. The downtown concentration has spread covering between freeways 10 and 60 and the interstate 5. The L. A. concentration is due to the enormous work availability in the garment districts and factories. This growth is also due to the number of Hispanics that have lived in Los Angeles all their lives. Long time residents of Los Angeles will sponsor and help relatives from other countries relocate in California. During the 60's, a second large group began to form in the Azusa Baldwin Park area, which spans the 210 and 605 freeways. Some other concentrations occur in the Southgate/Compton areas, along With Lakewood/Norwalk areas (cf. 1960's census tract chart).

he 1970's census tract chart demonstrates how much the Hispanic population grew and connected the major Los Angeles concentration spots and arteries. There is now an ink blob thick enough to cover all of the downtown area of Los Angeles, from just west of the 110 freeway, to just east of the 605, own the interstate 5, just north of the city of Norwalk. The Baldwin Park concentration has grown by at least 80%. There is a new concentration on the Pomona 60 covering the cities of La Puente and Industry.

There is another concentration beginning to flourish between Long Beach and San Pedro. This is probably due to the dock and harbor employment (cf. 1970's census chart).

The 1980's census tract continues to demonstrate just how fast the Hispanic population is growing in this area. Note that the downtown L. A. concentration is so large that it consumes East Los Angeles. Montebello, Pico Rivera, La Puente, Industry, all of Baldwin Park, Azusa, El Monte, Downey, South Gate, up to Vernon. There is a concentration in the area of Pomona, El Segundo, Torrance. Gardena, Carson, Santa Monica, Venice, north of Burbank, and in the south the entire area from San Pedro, to Carson, to Long Beach becomes saturated.

The projected 1990s census tract is probably misleading. By the growth of the previous four decades, it would suggest that there should be at least one third more of the black ink. The population demonstrated by these overlays do constitute that Hispanics represent over 50% of the population in the areas that is covered the black ink blobs. The Western Economic Research Co. Inc., obtained these results from the U.S. Census Bureau for decades of 1950, 1960, 1970, 1980 and up to 1985.

The projection of this report of the Hispanic community is alarming because America is receiving an enormous amount of documented and undocumented Hispanic people, coming from all over Mexico and the southern and central American countries. This influx is causing culture shock to the pre sent Hispanic churches and even to the incoming diversity of people. The Hispanic churches, no matter the denomination affiliation, are experiencing tremendous shock waves of many kinds. Everything from food, to style of music, slant of dialect, to level of economic need has paralyzed the average Hispanic church to the point of slowing it down to a crawl in the evangelism arena.

This is perhaps the hub of the trouble in reaching visitors in any Hispanic community. The diversity and challenge of this massive influx of different people with so many needs to attend to by the average Hispanic church is so overwhelming that pastors and their congregational members would rather stay inside their four wall-fortresses than face the problem. Due to the fact that the average Hispanic church cannot possibly meet the needs of such a wide range of people, the Hispanic church has pretty much stopped evangelizing. The need of some of these unchurched people is so bad that in some cases this situation becomes so detrimental that it pressures the

Hispanic church economically and causes the loss of membership to a point of exhaustion. The community that the Hispanic is in has probably undergone severe changes and the church has probably become totally unfamiliar with what is outside of its walls. The church has barely begun to experience what the changing community has been experiencing for decades.

Assessing Cultural Demands

Churches which were started in the 40's and 50's may today be witnessing its first or even second community change. The Hispanic church of the 40's and 50's was born in a traditional era, giving a powerful hold and draw on its members. This stands to reason why the Hispanic church has changed so little. Four decades of change have transpired since the 50's. Everybody else, the community, housing, markets, etc. changed with the times, not the church in general. The Hispanic church was founded by leaders that understood the needs of the people of their time. The Hispanic church needs to learn what its options are in today's market of drawing new visitors to church. To do nothing is to surely close its doors. Thankfully the Lord has provided gifted man and women who can offer suggestions of ways to grow. The church needs to rethink its strategy in how to use its limited resources.

Communities that have undergone changes have faced decade's transitions by learning who and how they can reach. Many times changes bring with them the answers needed. The church is no different than the secular world in trying to cope change. It just does it much slower. Change is often good. Too much change at once, though, can cause severe set backs. However, time has a way of shining light on things that need to change.

One such example of good change is the use of musical instruments now used in worship. In the early part of this century, most churches probably used a piano or air driven pipe organs. The Hispanic church possibly used a piano, a guitar or two, and maybe a set of drums. If the believers of those times could see the instruments used today to worship God, some might deem the church as too worldly. Time has helped the church utilize modem musical instruments and sound equipment. If today's young people had to worship using the instruments their parents used forty or fifty years ago, they would probably not play or even sing in the church.

This is what happened to some of the main-line denominations and their Baby Boomer children. The old guard or traditionalists of those denominations did not desire change, not even to keep their children and grand children because they were so strict with their ways of worshiping, they ended up losing the succeeding generations. Once one generation is lost, the children of the next generation are lost. Each generation must be allowed to worship in its own way. There is have an excellent example in Scripture to help in recognizing this dilemma.

In Judges 2:7 -10, there is a very interesting summary of what has happened to three generations of Israelites.

> "And the people served the Lord all the days of Joshua. And all the days of the elders that outlived Joshua, who had seen all the great works of the Lord, that he did for Israel. And Joshua the son of Nun, the servant of the Lord, died, being a hundred and ten years old. And they buried him in the border of his inheritance in Timnathheres, in the mount of Ephraim, on the north side of the hill of Gaash. And also all that generation were gathered unto their fathers: and there arose another generation after them, which knew not the Lord, nor yet the works which he had done for Israel."[6]

This passage explains what happened to three generations of people. The first generation saw God's miracles and strength in taking them out of Egypt. Their unbelief in God that He could give them anything they needed caused them to wander for forty years in the desert. This generation failed to believe and trust in the Lord and Died.

---

6 Judges 2:7-1(), Judge's explanation of what transpired in three generations.

The second generation was that of Joshua's age group This generation also had an opportunity to witness God's mighty works and His salvation for themselves and their children. This generation was unable to teach their children what God had done for them while taking over the promised land from the people who had it before they arrived. They spent much of their lives fighting the inhabitants of the promised land and building their homes, that they forgot to teach their children about God.

The result of two generation's unbelief and mistrust of the Lord caused a third generation to lose out completely. Scripture describes the third generation, or grandchildren of the people who left in the great exodus of Egypt, as a generation which did not know the Lord nor the works which He had done for Israel. The lack of teaching their children and grandchildren about God caused apostasy in Israel from then on.

Cultural demands and values do have an impact on the generations that follow. It is the direct responsibility of one generation to pass to the next the knowledge of reaching their own peers. Each generation has the responsibility to reach their own. The older generation has a responsibility to accept, nourish an communicate its willingness to help the younger generation.

DEMAND FOR CHOICES AND VARIETY

In today's world, there exist like never before societies of intercultural Hispanic differences which brings experiences of their likes and dislikes. In a time when it is culturally correct to ale one's own language, dress conforming to one's liking, and according to one's roots, different cultures of people are take advantage of the situation and selling in the market place very items needed to sustain such diversity.

An example of this is soda pop. Before the 50's, soda pop was purchased at an ice cream parlor. There were basically three choices: cola, uncola, and flavor drink such as orange or grape. Today, there is Coke: Classic Coke, Original Coke, Diet Coke, Caffeine Free Coke and Clear or zero Coke. The same goes for the other flavors like Pepsi, Doctor Pepper, and various un-colas.

Besides soda, ice cream was also purchased at the ice cream parlor. Like soda, there were not too many flavors to choose from. Now there are over three hundred flavors, not to mention yogurt, ice milk, and low Calorie ice-creams.

How about water? In the 50's, unless one was wealthy, it was plain tab water with ice. Today there is bottled water, mineral water, lemon water, and water with flavors like rasberry and peach. One must not forget water that is imported, purified, or flavored with a vegetable or fruit.

If one stops at supermarkets, all one has to do is to go down the aisles to see just how much these stores are trying to persuade all the people of its communities to come and shop there. Anybody can shop in these stores and buy ingredients to cook Asian dinners, Mexican meals, black food, American dishes, and frozen T. V. foods, to mention a few.

In these same supermarket a person can find a vegetable and fruit stand, a meat market, I delicatessen, a bakery shop, a fish counter, a pharmacy, hardware, cosmetics, a branch of a local bank to do banking needs, and even areas to design postcards. Now, why are supermarkets and other stores trying so hard to outsell themselves in such wide variety of goods to the various ethnic groups in these communities?

They have come to realize that cultural awareness and sensitivity to the variety of ethnics can attract and retain customers. It is a lesson the church needs to learn if it, too, plans to stay healthy and continue to bring the lost to Christ. The church has to assimilate such a strategy of entering the diverse changes that now exist in most communities.

ACTION STEPS

1. Assess the ministry area from a perspective of people
who know nothing about the Gospel. Assume that the people being reached are completely unchurched and have no clue as to the extent of knowledge of the Gospel or of Christ. This in turn will cause the church to present the Gospel in its simplest and purest form.

2. Assess the ministry area from a perspective of having conceived ideas of where the unchurched it is trying to reach lives. Again assume the worst. Try to prepare the church with material and training in reaching any and all type of people in all types of languages. Map out an area of 12 to 30 miles in diameter of the territory believed to be the ministry area. The distance above depends on if it is an urban or rural ministry area. Plot the ministry area on a map, make copies of it to all workers. Make transparencies of it and show the congregation where they have to be on the look out for possible sites for ministry.

3. Assess the ministry area from a perspective of having no preconceived idea of what type of music and

worship styles will need. As the members or evangelists are mapping out the areas have them listen to the music the people are enjoying the styles of programs they hear. This may lead to an under standing of what type of music that area might enjoy.

4. Assess the ministry area from a perspective of having no idea of the kind of leaders it will need. This action step is more difficult than the others. Some people will follow just about anyone, and others will only follow their own kind. It is the same with witnessing and being invited. Some people will come no matter who calls on them. Others will only come if their own came to invite them. Have the personnel who is doing the mapping pay close attention to this area when they are out doing their work.

Summary

Assessing a community has many advantages. The church is assessing can actually get a suitable feel as to what that particular area of ministry needs in order to make it better. By far, stores who do their homework in targeting an area in which they wish to build a store will find that they will have more success. The same is for the church. The church that does its homework well will get good results.

Reader's Notes

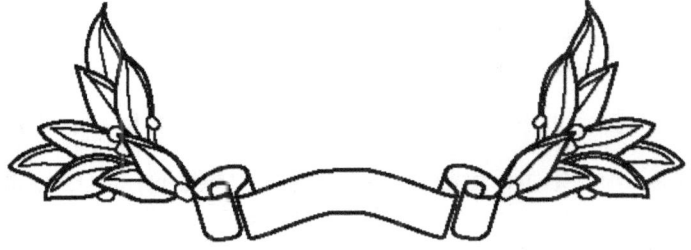

CHAPTER FIVE
GENERATIONAL CONTOURS AND THEIR EFFECTS
GENERATIONAL IDEOLOGY

It has been advantageous to those who have learned what generational ideology can mean for the church in reaching people. Generational ideology is the study of the people who were born in certain time periods. It is the understanding of what binds people of certain time periods to each other. Time and What transpires in it influences ideologies, values, decisions, events, and people. The Scriptures identify the use of the word "generations" when speaking about events, people, or creations in a given time period.

Scripture mentions the word generations four times. The first is when it speaks of creation:

> "These are the generations of the heavens and of the earth when they were created, in the day that the Lord God made the earth and the heavens, and every plant of the field before it was in the earth, and every herb of the field before it grew: for the Lord God had not caused it to rain upon the earth, and there was not a man to till the ground.!"[1]

When Scripture speaks of the time it took to create the heavens, the earth, and the elements therein, it uses the

---

[1] Genesis 2:4-5, Creations's explanation of generations.

word generations. Generations here speak not of man, but of the plants the herbs of the field. What does the word generations have to do with plants and herbs in the field? It is believed that the word generations has to do with the offspring of the plants and herbs in the form of its seeds. The entire book of Genesis is viewed from the standpoint of generations by Matthew in his in the first verse.

Charles John Ellicott in his commentary on the Bible says this when comparing Matthew's use of the word generations in view of Christ's genealogy and the first book of the Bible: "This title, ever, does not mean a genealogical list of a person's ancestors, but the register of his posterity. As applied to the 'heavens and the earth' it signifies the history of what followed upon their creation."[2]

There is another portion of Scripture that ought to be considered in the book of Genesis. It is found in chapter nine verse twelve: "And God said, This is the token of the covenant which I make between me and you and every living creature that is with you, for perpetual generations."[3]

---

[2] Charles John Ellicott, Ellicott's Bible Commentary, Grand Rapids, Mich: Zondervan Publishing House,1971), pg. 7.

[3] Genesis 9:12, God's covenant with Noah and all living creatures and their generations.

God made a covenant with Noah, his descendants, every living creature, and the earth that He would not destroy the earth again by water. God also included their perpetual generations in this covenant. It is the understanding that the word generations here is for people, living creatures, and plant life.

Twice in the Gospel of Matthew, Jesus uses the word generation. The first is in chapter twelve verse thirty-four where He calls the Pharisees a generation of snakes. The other is in chapter twenty-four verse thirty-four where He states that "this generation" shall not pass until all the things He has been talking about would come to pass. Both times that Jesus uses the word generation He uses it in reference to a certain period of time in which people lived. Thus, it seems appropriate at this time to consider generations that are currently alive today.

GENERATIONS OF TODAY

A book by William Strauss and Neil Howe entitled **Generations** is highly recommend for reading. This book offers much information in helping to understand what will attract visitors. Simply stated, the more known about who is trying to be reached, the easier it becomes to reach them.

Strauss and Howe describe their work thus:

> "This book presents the "history of the future" by narrating a recurring dynamic of generational behavior that seems to determine how and when we participate as individuals in social change-or social upheaval. We say, in effect that this dynamic repeats itself. This is reason enough to make history important: For if the future replays the past, so too must the past anticipate the future." 4

Their concept is to study the generational behavior of famous people of certain periods of time. Strauss and Howe have developed a life-cycle course that people in generations go through. This is the way state it:

> "We retell a favorite old tale in a brand-new way: the full story of America from the Puritans forward, presented along what we call the "generational diagonal"-the life cycle course, childhood through old age, lived by the discrete birth year groups we define as "generations." We identify eighteen such generations through four centuries of American history, dating back to the first New World colonists. Among these generations, we find important recurring personality patterns-specifically, four types of "peer personalities" that have (in all but one case) followed each other in a fixed order. We call this repeating pattern the "generational cycle.' II The cycle lies at the heart of our story and offers, we believe, an important explanation for why the story of America unfolds as it does."5

---

4 William Strauss, and Niel Howe,. <u>Generations: The History of Americans's Future</u> (New York, N.Y.: Williams Morrow & Company, Inc., 1991), pg. 8.

5 strauss and Howe, pg. 8

One of the eighteen generations that they speak about belongs to each reader of this dissertation no matter what the age. In this chapter, only the material relevant with the generational cycles that are still alive today will be offered. In all, there have only been five generational cycles and eighteen generations:

Table 1.-- Five cycles of Generations starting in 1584 and ending sometime after the turn of the second millennium.

THE GENERATIONAL CYCLE IN AMERICA [6]

Colonial	Revolutionary	Civil War	Great Power	Millennial
1584-1700	1701-1791	1792-1859	1860-1942	1943-2026
Puritans	Awakening	Transcendental	Missionary	Boomers
Cavalier	Liberty	Gilded	Lost	Busters
Glorious	Republican	Progressive	G. I.	Boomlet
Enlightenment	Compromise	---------	Silent	Not born yet

LIVING GENERATIONS IN AMERICA

The material analyzed will be on the latter half of the power generational cycle and on most of the millennial generational cycle. Some of the material discussed in this section on some of the generations will be brief, while other

---

[6] Strauss and Howe, pg. 57.

Generations will be be studied more in depth.

Table 2.--Five living generations starting with the G.I.s and ending with the Boomlet generation.

The following are the living American generations: 7

"G. I."	Elders	born 1901-24	age 71 to 94
"Silent"	mid lifers	born 1925-42	age 58 to 70
"Boomers"	rising adults	born 1943-60	age 35 to 52
"Busters"	Youths	born 1961-81	age 14 to 34
"Boomlet"	Children	born 1982-2?	age 12- to ?

Each generational cycle has a maximum of four generations in it. Some have only three due to abrupt changes. Each generation has a type with which it is identified. There are only four types and they repeat themselves in every generational cycle. These types are idealist, reactive, civic, and adaptive.

Chapter three mentioned of three generations beginning from the time of Moses. From the calling of Moses to the grandchildren of Joshua was a generational cycle. This generational cycle could very well be named 'Exodus' or 'Called Out'. At any rate, the four types can be identified via the Bible. The first was the Idealist which began with God preparing and calling Moses, of which his

---

7 Strauss and Howe, pg. 97.

brother and sister, Aaron and miriam, are part.

The next generation is the Reactive who reacted by building the golden calf. The third generation is the Civic who birthed the generals Joshua and Caleb. The last generation is the Adaptive generation which Judges chapter two speaks about as not knowing the Lord and all the works that He did for Israel. Just as in the time of Moses there were multiple succeeding generations of Israelites, so it is today. As seen on the previous chart, there currently are five living generations to evangelize with the Gospel of the Lord Jesus Christ.

There also is a generational cycle in the era of the kings. It starts out with King Saul, reigning 40 years. Next comes David who reigns for forty years until his son Solomon takes over. Solomon's reign lasts forty years also when he dies. Next comes both kings Rehoboam and Jeroboam, who end up dividing the kingdom in two. Generational cycles have a tendency to swing like a pendulum, back and forth from one extreme to the other. Generations have always existed and can be used by the church to help it understand who is currently living and how they might be reached.

Fig. 10. The diagram below is an extension of previous models to maintain continuity of thought and is illustrated by author. Both diagrams demonstrate repetitive cycles that the Hebrew nation went through in different times in their history.

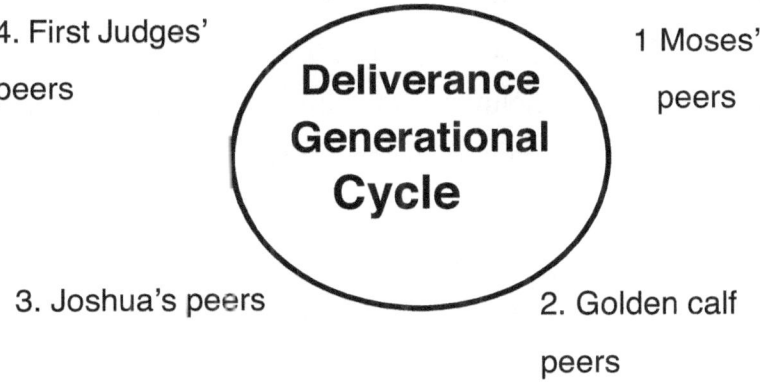

Fig. 11. The diagram below is an extension of previous models to maintain continuity of though and is illustrated by author.

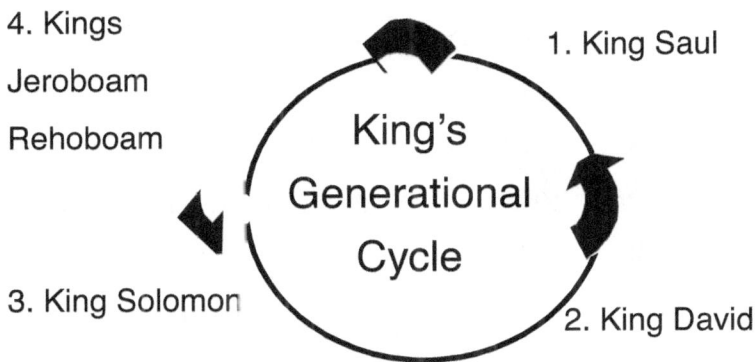

The five living generations today are very different in character and values. They present to the church a wide variety of considerations when reaching them with the Gospel. The more that is known about each generation and its values and principles, the better the strategy can be planned for any church to be effective in reaching them. There is sufficient material for all people and ages to uncover solutions to attract and retain visitors for almost every church in the United States of America. Some could say that the proposed concept is too complicated for the average church to undertake with its current resources. What if the church had a firm idea, more or less, as to when the tribulation period was to happen? Would not this encourage it to channel all its resources to obtain as much information as possible for the unchurched masses?

Strauss and Howe predict through their research that the States of America is going to go through a serious crises as early as 2010 and as late as 2020. By 2010 there will be no more of the elder or 'G. I.' Generation, and the oldest, the "Silent" generation would be 85 years to 92 years of age. This standing generation would have picked up the generation which follows the "Boomlet" generation. Not much has happened to change the main group of these generations, to understand and create a sound program in reaching these generations would be well spent.

It is a well known fact that America is fast becoming a nation that is losing its Christian foundation. It truly is a fertile mission field for any religion, Christian or otherwise. What began as a nation looking for freedom to worship God in any form without the fear of a government reprisal has become a nation enmeshed in materialism and sin. The "Time of Grace" will be ending as a nation that does not understand how or who to reach with the Gospel. Unless something is done, the result will be a nation and a generation that is godless like the one in the second chapter of Judges. This is the whole reason for writing this work: That God may help pastors and churches find what they need in order to bring to Christ to as many souls as possible.

GENERATIONAL DESCRIPTIONS

G. I. GENERATION

The reason to include the following material of the generational descriptions of the today's generations is so that the church and especially the Hispanic church can have an idea of how this information can help.

The G. I. Generation is a powerful era of people born

between 1901-1924. During their time of leadership, they left some remarkable stamps on America's social, economic, and political establishments. The "G. I." grew up in a time produced by the first World War. This generation is looked upon and regarded as strong and constructive. This was a rationalistic and civic generation that had everything a generation could want--a strong family unit and opportunities for success. Time seemed to move in a much more gentle pace and changes happened slower during this generation. Ideals and traditions which were passed down by their parents (the Lost Generation) and grandparents (the Missionary Generation) were never questioned as to their relevance in their time. Thus, for the "G.1." Generation it would be natural to think that their children (the Boomers) should also accept the norms and traditions set before them by their parents and grandparents.

Unfortunately, the Boomer children did not view the changes that followed with the same perspectives. The fast pace of life has revealed one thing: that change is constant in this world. Many G.I.ers have had a hard time understanding younger generations, due to the fact that these younger generations do not always see the world through the same eyes of experience.

In order for a church to launch a program of evangelism, visitation, or attraction of the "G.I." Generation, the leadership of any church must consider the profile of its church. The church must ask itself questions pertaining to the overall appeal of the way it does church in relationship to the way "G.1.s' enjoy church. The church should research such areas as the worship style that "G.I.s" would enjoy. What kind of message would be challenging? What ministries would they join? An easy way to view this is to think of the kind of church the Boomer's grandparents would have attended.

SILENT GENERATION

The Silent generation, born between the years of 1925-1942, is a soft-spoken era which grew up during F. D. Roosevelt's time as President and set between two World Wars. It also saw one of the hardest economic times in the United States, the Great Depression. This generation saw, heard, and lived virtues and values of two great generations of men and women before them. They lived in an uneasy and uncertain times. This is a generation that can adapt to most anything. It was Teddy Roosevelt who first spoke to this generation as living during the era of the "Melting Pot of America." It was then believed that all people who migrated to the United States would become one People and one nation.

Both Teddy Roosevelt and the Silent generation never dreamed that the Melting Pot concept would never succeed. They believed that whoever came to this nation would learn to assimilate into it Unfortunately, this was not the case. The Silent generation never imagined that today we would call it a "Salad Bowl" with its great variety of dressings.

What happened to this generation during its time to govern in the work and world scene also happened to them in the religious area. They were the adaptive generation that should have been able to adapt their view of work, world events and also church policy to accommodate the changes coming to them as this world entered its millennial perspectives. Their failure to adapt to the changes needed around them had major impacts to the respective areas.

In the work arena, the failure came in resisting change in retooling from an industrial era to a scientific era. The fruits of this resistance were evident when steel and auto-making factories went broke.

Table 3.-- The following are generations are from the Great Power & Millennial Generational Cycles:

"G. I."	Civics	born 1901-1924
"Silent"	Adaptive	born 1925-1942
"Boomers"	Idealists	born 1946-1964
"Busters"	Reactive	born 1965-1985
"Boomlet"	Civics	born 1986-2011
"Millennial"	Adaptive	born 2012-2024

In the religious area, the silent generation failed to be adaptive and continued the growth of the church through meeting the needs of the next generation, the Boomers. Instead of adapting, they fortified themselves even stronger in their parents' and grandparents' religious values and systems of worship and evangelism, not transitioning the work of God in the church from traditional methods/views to idealist/millennial ways. Thus we have a break in the generational cycle because of the strength and power certain generations bring with them.

In terms of religion, this quiet, highly adaptable generation has a greater ease in adapting to various forms of worship when former generational pressure is not present. They are able to worship in a structured liturgical style, as well as in a methodical environment, or even in the contemporary structure found in today's churches. They are a hard working group and easy to please.

They like to live with their families and help out their neighbors.

THE BABY BOOM GENERATION

The Boomer generation, which began in 1943 and lasted to 1964, is probably the largest number of people to have been born in a single generation. Their parents who were from the Silent generation saw the Boomer era as a gifted generation in many respects. They have the capability to be the founders great wealth for all of mankind if they will, but need to mat out of their self-centeredness. They need to learn that the whole world does not revolve around them. Their sheer numbers the power of their creative and innovative minds and ideals, if channeled correctly, can help mankind all over the globe.

Growing up in a postwar era in a country not ravished by war has given the Boomer generation a boost into a world selfish materialism, and profitable gain in comparison to the rest of the world. Generations with men and women such as the G.I.s or Boomers are found all over the world, not just in the United States alone. Most countries in this world have their own versions of generational groups. In most countries the generational groups may take longer to develop and grow due to the pace of the changing times. Because of the pace, the difference between back to back generations are more easily adjusted and accepted.

In comparing the rate of change in our country to that of other countries we can see that generational changes in groups in this country will mature much faster, causing major differences and even conflict from father to son generations. The question has to be asked, what is causing the rapid changes in America that is not happening in other countries? Now some say that the rapid growth and fast changing times started after the Civil War, yet, I believe that it was spawn in Europe and caused countless generations of people to seek a world in which they could grow such an idea, thus America was born and was design by a need to be free and do whatever it took and whatever it wanted. Many other countries have tried to assimilate America's work ethic, music, freedom, and a generous style of living.

Yet of all the previous generations in America, the generation with the greatest change came with the Boomers. Their childhood was simple, with a life of sports and family. As a generation, they have not suffered pain, hunger, the loss of parents, home, or security. To the contrary, they have had a peaceful life and many educational opportunities. Unlike their G.I. (grandparents) or their Silent generation (parents), they have not struggled with many of the problems that other generations have had in comparison to theirs. The size of their generations, the giftedness of their peers, and the wealth of their times have created an environment steeped in the desire to acquire all the possessions this life can give. All of these elements in the Boomer era have produced a generation of self-centered, uncaring adults.

The Boomers believe that in their circle they possess a unique vision that has set many things in motion from the very moment that they were born. Due to their sheer numbers and available collective wealth that their parents have provided, the commercial markets have, from their infancy, catered to them. As they matured into their teenage years, they found out that within their ranks they had rich talent that could very easily influence industries in the areas of music, sports, clothing, language terminology, and even the movie (Hollywood) industry. Radio and television stations began to sponsor many programs for this generation. This catering and pampering have caused this generation to develop a lifestyle of moral selfishness and greed. Because of this, Boomers spend more than what they earn, and live today on tomorrow's paycheck.

This lifestyle will continue until something happens to show this generation the outcome of its moral dilemma.

For the most part, the Boomers thought that their lifestyles, their strength and ambition to get rich quick would bring them happiness; but, instead, it has only brought them monetary problems and marital/family chaos. The price of attaining high economic goals in their lives has produced a generation of very lonely children, split marriages, and single parenting. What started out to be a life full of love, happiness, joy, and prosperity has lead, for the most part, to despair.

The parents of Boomers, for the most part, were Christian and the children of Christians. Most of the Boomers can recall the previous two generations as being devoted to country, God and church. The differences in the Boomers' personalities's needs and behavior distanced them from their parents' and grandparents' religious heritage. The Boomers, for the most part, are not against God or the church. It is merely that they find the church's style of morality and worship somewhat stuffy and interfering with what the Boomers cherish the most- their play time. Add to this their parent's silent acquiescence in permissive education and the Boomers' unwillingness to curb their appetite for recreational enjoyment, and the result is a generation that sees the church and all it stands for a bit of a bore, out of sync with their wants, and out of date with some vague idea of what a church ought to represent.

Today, the traditional mainline church plays less and less a major role in Boomers' lives. When mainline churches lost the grip on the Boomer children, they not only lost one generation, but the succeeding generations as well. Not being sensitive and aware of this generation's needs for spiritual growth is one of the greatest tragedies today's church have allowed to transpire. Never has a generation produced so many superstars, singing groups, famous movie stars, and teenage idols. Imagine what might have been accomplished if the mainline churches had foreseen the talent that could have been brought into the church.

The fact that the church in general has not been able to reach the Boomer generation has caused it to rely on the older generations and migrating groups for its sporadic growth. The Boomers that did continue their spiritual growth with God either stayed with the church or left her to start para-church organizations. The ones who stayed in traditional churches adapted to what continued to be the traditional paradigms. Many of Boomers who left the mainline churches founded such organizations as the

Navigators, Teen Challenge, Youth for Christ, and other such para-church organizations.

The growth of para church organizations came about to fulfill the two great needs. The first was to reach the Boomer Generation which would not have been possible through the old traditional mainline churches. The second need was to allow Boomer Christians to achieve a call to ministry and missions as they saw it fit their own generation. They saw the Boomer generation as unreachable with the typical-traditional ways of worship, programs and activities that the mainline churches had. The para-church organizations were created for the sole purposes of witnessing, evangelizing, and counseling troubled youth. Attracting these lost and misguided souls to Christ was their message. They were never founded or organized to keep and nourish new converts. The need to fill that void came from churches like the Eagles' Nest and Calvary Chapels.

These new churches were able to grow at an outstanding rate because of the style of worship and message they brought. Mainline and independent churches that wish to tap brought. Mainline and independent churches that wish to tap into this large number of Boomers might want to consider changing their current style of church business.

The G. I. generation left such a strong influence on church procedure and style of arrangement in worship and music that their children, the Silent Generation thought it a sin to change anything. When traditional churches failed to understand the spiritual needs of the Boomers to change some things in their worship services to accommodate the Boomers's spiritual needs and instead foresaw the change as a major shift of how they had been ministering in their worship services for years, they felt that the sacrifice was to great in the changing of what they had come to hold as sacred.

BABY BUSTER GENERATION

The Buster generation includes those children born between the years 1964 through 1985. That is the generation which came after the Boomers and is typically called "Baby Bust" generation. The reason that the Busters have been given this name is because of the birth rate or sheer numbers born during their generation. The difference in numbers is somewhere around one half to one third depending on who has done the of study demographics. If viewing the quantity of Boomers to that of Busters as balloons, the Busters developed a 33%-50% leak in the balloon. Thus the term "bust" for Busters. The size, resources, and attention created by the Boomer Generation has overshadowed anything the Buster generation has done. This has led demographers to state that the Busters generation has not had an effect like its predecessors. The Buster Generation is approximately two-thirds the size of the Boomer generation in numbers and has clearly not demons trated the giftedness or wealth that the Boomer generation has displayed.

The Busters are the children from two different generations. They are from the late child bearing years of the Silent generation. They also come from early and mid-Boomers parents. Depending who has birthed this generation, there tends to be a strong difference in the makeup of the Busters. Busters whose parents are the Silent generation have a tendency to have fewer problems in adapting to the work force and daily problems of life. Those Busters whose parents have been the Boomers have tougher problems in adapting and handling life issues and problems. This generation has seen labeled with various negative connotation and generation X. They have been lumped in with mall rats, drug gangs, collegians cannot find Chicago on the map. They have been labeled dumb, greedy, soulless, lazy, and carefree. This is the generation which coined the phrase "latchkey children." It should be noted that latch-key children came only from Boomer parents and not from Silent parents. For the most part this generation (latchkey children/Busters) has a chip on their shoulders towards the Boomer generation. They feel that the Boomers have always had it easy, whereas the Busters have had to work harder to succeed.

The Busters feel that the Boomers will finish off consuming everything and leave nothing for them. Sometimes the relationship of Boomers and Busters are blurred due to the age difference. At other times they are as close as father and son. Whatever the relationship the Boomer has with the Buster, whether it is an older brother or a father, it is one that will often be at odds. These bad feelings between the two generations will be an obstacle to overcome when ministering the Gospel.

BOOMLETS OR MILLENNIAL CHILDREN

The Boomlet children are the generation who will be teenagers at the turn of the second millennium, those children born from 1985, and those who will continue to be born just after the turn of the second millennium. The term Boomlet has been given to these children because the bulk of their generation will be children fathered from the mid to late Boomers. The early married Buster generation will also contribute to this group. It is believed that the Boomlet generation is going to surpass the quality of the Busters, but not quite as large as the Boomer. Because Boomlets are being birthed by both Boomer and Buster generations, the combined generations can contribute to a larger Boomlet number born due strictly to their parents numbers. Thus combined numbers of the Boomers and the Busters formed a major element in the size of the Boomlet birth rate in their generation. This phenomenon is unlike the Boomers' birth rate. The Boomer parents were having four to six or more children per household. In the Boomlet generation, the household number of births is one to three. Thus the name "boom" - because of the size of their generation and "let" because of the outlet into the new Millennium.

Because the Boomlet children come from two generational sources, they will be reared by two very different mind sets. This will cause the Boomlets in time to be viewed as a split generation. Part of the children born in this generation will have been reared by successful, well off Boomers who waited until they had reached affluence. The other part of the children of this generation will have been reared by Busters who already feel like "Johnnies-come-lately" in the job market place.

There is very little information on this group because the oldest was eleven years old in 1996. However, this generation will probably prove to be an interesting one. Leaders of churches need to learn all that they can about the generations to which they belong, for it will help them understand themselves and their peers better.

People living today are perhaps in the fastest, most hectic paced time period known to date. From the 1960's through 1990s, Americans have rumbled through their resources, people, morals, and lifestyles. This rumbling will not cease; it will continue to develop and rage out of control. The church can either close its ears and pretend that the Lord will come soon and take what remains in the church to heaven, or it can open up its doors to all that is going on around it and begin to deal with it.

HISPANIC GENERATIONS VALUES

Dr. Morris Massey is the author of a profile called Values Analysis Profile. I have used this profile extensively in the field to help pastors and leaders identify with their values. I have discovered that the generational cycles are very much tied to their values, which have in turn given these generations their identity. Generations are motivated by the values which have been inbred by forces around them, and not necessarily by their parents.

It is believed that a child identifies early on in his childhood with most of his values with which he will be making adult decisions.

The value of my using the Value Profile was to help the pastors and leaders see where they obtained their value system. Different ages obtain their value system according to where They were growing up. The following drawing will demonstrate what we are saying.

Fig. 12. The diagram below is an illustration to demonstrate the forces that affect our Value system. Illustration by author.

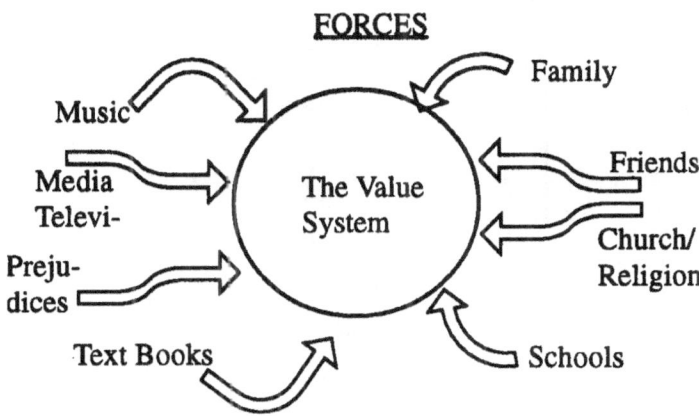

These forces are the main elements that produce in each generation the necessary values in which they will grow up believing and trusting. These forces are carried over from generation to generation. The following drawing will further demonstrate this principle.

Fig. 13. The drawing below is an illustration to demonstrate the four value systems in the form of individuals.

The Traditionalist   The Synthesizer
         The Inbetweener   The challenger

The drawing at the bottom of the previous page are of the four boys who represent four value systems. They are from left to right; the Traditionalists, the Inbetweeners, the Challengers, and the Synthesizers. The first value system termed the Traditionalists is very powerful and influential core value system. They hold a lot of influence in their adherents because this group was embedded with many values from the 1920's through the 1940's. Some of the influencing factors were World War 1 and 2, the Great Depression, mobility, and the family. Security played an important part in the Traditionalists lives.

The next value system is the Inbetweeners. Their value systems were embedded into them during the late 1940's through the 1950s. The Inbetweener's value system stands between two powerful value systems that are pulling in opposite directions. The two value systems are the Traditionalist and the Challengers. They feel that they are always caught in the middle. They either stand with their fathers and their grandfather's traditions and lose finishing with their peers, or they become outsiders and renegades to the old family because they side with the Challengers. For them it is a no-win situation; either way they lose. Most Inbetweeners generally will dedicate themselves to their Work and family life, and end up leaving scenes where they are used as pawns. Because they tend to run away, they end up with Conflicting perspectives of individual responsibility and individual expression.

The third value system is the Challengers-better known as Rejectionists. Their value system were embedded in them from mid 1950s through the early 1970's. These challengers are the bulk of the post World War baby boom. Since we have already talked about this group before, it need not be mentioned

The fourth value system is the Synthesizers, and they were programmed in the mid 1970's and later. This is the leading edge "now" generation who has been influenced tremendously by diverse and sometimes conflicting values of the proceeding generation clusters. The Synthesizers emerge as skeptical, concerned, and a conservative learning group. They recognize contemporary problems are complex and older solutions and methods do not always work. Perhaps their most positive attributes are their behavior to be able to adapt and renegades to the old family because they side with the Challengers. For them it is a no-win situation; either way they lose. Most Inbetweeners generally will dedicate themselves to their

Work and family life, and end up leaving scenes where they are used as pawns. Because they tend to run away, they end up with Conflicting perspectives of individual responsibility and individual expression.

The third value system is the Challengers-better known as Rejecticnists. Their value system were embedded in them from mid 1950s through the early 1970's. These challengers are the bulk of the post World War baby boom. Since we have already talked about this group before, it need not be mentioned

The fourth value system is the Synthesizers, and they were programmed in the mid 1970's and later. This is the leading edge "now" generation who has been influenced tremendously by diverse and sometimes conflicting values of the proceeding generation clusters. The Synthesizers emerge as skeptical, concerned, and a conservative learning group. They recognize contemporary problems are complex and older solutions and methods do not always work. Perhaps their most positive attributes are their behavior to be able to adapt in fast changing times, and to be able to accept change as the norm, and to be able to use their potential resourcefulness.

The reason to go through all of this information again is to be able to see the complexity of the challenge that the aver age church, has in attracting and retaining visitors. Yet for the average Hispanic church, the problems surmount even higher. They have to contend with America's fast changing values, and at the same time try to keep in pace with the incoming masses of migrating people. For the most part, the average migrant workers that come from outside of the United States are going to be Traditionalists. As these people come into the United States, they either are going to blend with the rest, or reject this nation and eventually go back to their home country. This is what Mary Ballesteros-Coronel was reporting about in chapter two. Many of the migrating undocumented worker will not stay and will be forced by the value systems of this country to return to wherever they came from.

These undocumented workers that return again to their own lands will usually stay in the United States for the a minimum of two years and not more than ten. Most of these undocumented workers never bring their families, for fear that their children may like it here and not want to go back again.

They, on the other hand, go back and forth between these countries boasting of the money that they have made. This influences the children, and when they are

Old enough they too decide to venture out to this country.

Reporter Ballesteros-Coronel reports that between 1982 through 1993 more than half of those that came into this country returned in less than two years, and more than 70% returned in less than ten years. I requested from the Apostolic Assembly in the Faith of Christ Jesus, a predominant corporation of churches, some documents from their files to see how this exodus could have affected their churches during that same time.

To my surprise, it had affected their total number of membership over-all. In their 1976-1994 membership report from their 1994 convention, this report shows that in 1978-1980 their numbers were climbing to all high in their ability to attract and retain new members and the numbers had soared to 60.67% in those years, yet they knew not what was causing this spike. By 1982 when the Instituto de Asuntos Publicos California (PPIC) had begun tracking the undocumented immigrants for a ten year period, the Apostolic Assembly had already begun to drop from 60.67% to 16.17%, nearly 3/4% of their overall outreach and retention. Between the years of 1984 and 1986, the spike seemed to have dropped another 50%. By 1988, they had reached a low of -0.21 of their ability to reach, attract, and retain new members. It was not until 1990 that they began to climb once again. Though the percentages that were taken from the records of the Apostolic Assembly are nation wide for them, and the tracking that was done by PPIC was for California only, it does not invalidate this discovery.

The PPIC report only showed what is happening in California. However, what is happening in California is happening in all of the United States. The mentality of the immigrants to not stay here no more than two years is a cultural and ethnic decision. That is, these people have no real interest of migrating permanently. They only come for the wages then return home again.

Reporter Ballesteros-Coronel gave additional numbers in her report. She stated in her article that during the years of 1980 through 1990, a sum of 3.2 million that entered California, an average of 326,495 per year, about 29% or 100,000 stayed par year during those 10 years in the 1980's. The rest, some 226,495, returned within a two year period.

Reporter Ballesteros-Coronel reports also that 74% of the undocumented workers that entered this country are men who came alone, 12% came with their families, and 9.5% had their children over here. It is true, then Hispaic church minis try areas are impacted with tremendous numbers of people coming that will not stay more than two years. For the average Hispanic church with its limited resources, it could find itself ministering to a hungry population that is highly unstable in their residences. This maybe a factor why the Hispanic church sees a tremendous turn-around in their numbers yearly. They are constantly reaching, attracting, and baptizing, but do not seem to grow very much in the long run. This type of growth drains the church, its resources and its leadership constantly, to the point of exhaustion and burn-out. The average Hispanic church has the ability to reach a better and more stable crowd, but they are going to have to do their home-work as far as where and with whom they want to spend their resources.

HISPANIC GENERATIONS

The drawing at the bottom of this page illustrates Massey's typically value system chart, only modified with Hispanics instead. These pictures can represent any migrating people from Hispanic or non-Hispanic countries.

Fig. 14. The diagram below is an extension of previous models to maintain continuity of thought and is illustrated by author. It is a combined picture of the four Hispanic Generations from all of the Latin countries including Mexico that have crossed the northern Mexican borders into the United States seeking economical growth.

HISPANIC GENERATIONS

Hispanic Generations

Traditionalist

Inbetweener

Challenger

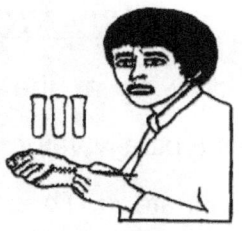
Synthesizer

Those undocumented workers that do decide to stay in this country will reject the current value system and isolate themselves from it as best that as can. They will seek out areas that offer them work, housing, similar foods, activities, friends, newspapers, television programs, literature, schools, and a church I they feel meets their own value system. Because they decided to stay here, their children automatcally become influenced by the current cultures and value systems.

Fig. 15. The drawing below is that of Massey's chart Traditionalist, only with a Hispanic characters, instead of a white person.

THE TRADITIONALIST

Depending when they migrated to this country, they may encounter in their lifetimes some or most of the value systems that have plagued our society with changes. In the above drawing the "Hispanic Traditionalist" who came into North America looking primarily for work is presented. Note the simple clothing and tools from their native country used to represent their Traditionalist way of life. They sought only to work and earn I way of living, so as to bring up their children having more than what they had growing up.

Their way of life is very simple, from their foods to their clothing, and what they want out of life. They seek peace, tranquility and freedom to go back and forth to their native lands to visit their family and friends. They will instill their value systems on their children, only to find out that as they stay here longer and their children are influenced more by the new values. As their children grow, even in barrios or Hispanic communities with the old countries foods, clothing, music, culture, language, and people, the children will learn the new ways. The children will adapt to the new subculture and its value system, the new food, clothing, new language, the new Hispanic look to the point that the parents will soon not understand why their children rebel against them and the old ways.

Fig. 16. The following drawing is that of Massey's chart the Inbetweener, only with a Hispanic.

THE INBETWEENER

The Hispanic Inbetweener generation is that value system which was born in Mexico or some other country, but the Inbetweener generation moved to this country at a very young age with his parents or alone. He has a mix of values and memories from both the old country as well as of this new one. He has no real friends to speak of, only relatives and people that he has because they are rom the old country. If he does have friends, they are probably from his work. If his parents are seniors citizens then they probably live with him. He is most likely a legal resident and has probably applied for legal citizenship. He has no formal education, except that which he has been able to get in the United States. He works in one of three areas of employment: agriculture, construction, or some sort of mechanical trade. As an adult he does not share with his parents the notion of going back to Mexico or some other country. In fact, he does not join them when they visit friends and family. He feels that there is nothing in the old country for him. He probably married in the States, and most of his children were born here. He has wrestled with his former and new value systems, and is currently confuse about what he believes. He does not understand his wife and even less his children. He is the one who feels that he is" in between, like he does not belong. Sometimes he just wishes he could leave everything behind. There are still some small similarities between the dress style of the Inbetweener and the Traditionalist. Sometimes he just wishes he could leave everything behind. There are still some small similarities between the dress style of the Inbetweener and the Traditionalist.

Sometimes he just wishes he could leave everything behind. There are still some small similarities between the dress style of the Inbetweener and the Traditionalist.

The third system of values is by far the most challenging because they are the ones that desire to change things, but the fact, is, they do not really know what to do or what to make changes to make.

Fig. 17. The following drawing is that of Massey's chart of the Challenger, only with a Hispanic instead of a white person.

THE CHALLENGER

The Challenger value system produces change. Though sometimes change is good, the Challenger never actually knows whether the changes that he is asking for is really all that good, to self or others. All they know is that something within them is driving them to pursue change. This value system is the agent by which traditional chords are broken. This is the generation that has seen and heard stories of the horrors that their parents, grandparents and people have suffered getting to this place. They see their parents' and grandparents styles of living, and they want more. It is this value system which most people call the second generation. It is the most difficult generation to reach with the Gospel.

These Challengers are usually the youngest children born to the older Traditional parents. They can also be the oldest children born to the Inbetweeners. At any rate, they are legally, born in the United States. They are Hispanic children who grew up running up and down the barrio streets with no fear of the immigration taking them away. This is the reason that they are able to stand in the fields to organize and walk in marches.

The fourth value system is by far the one that can blend with all of the other three value systems. This is generally the educated value system who moves away from the barrio to pursue their dreams.

THE SYNTHESIZER

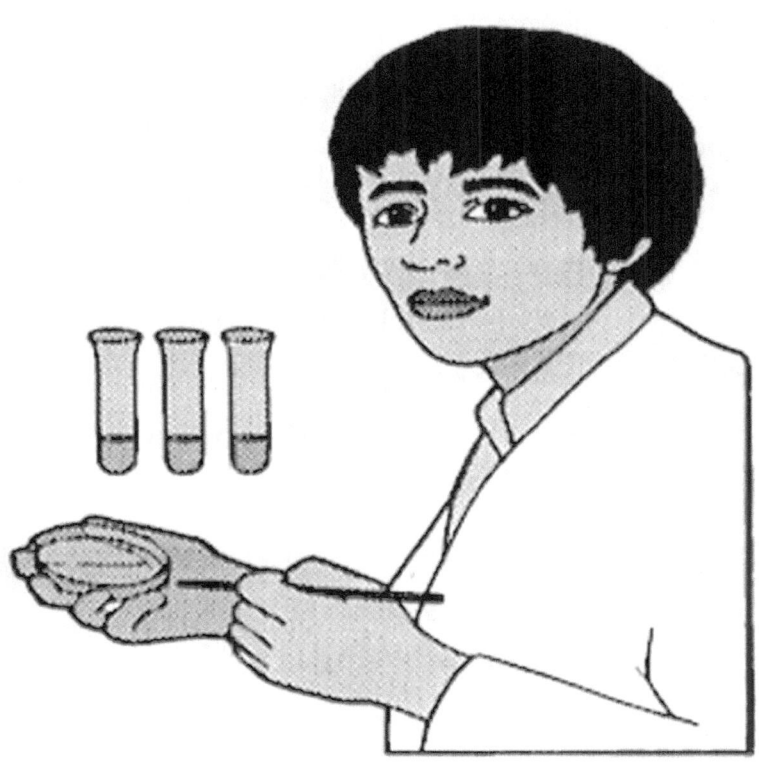

The Synthesizers are those who wish to integrate themselves with others. Their main fear is the lack of personal congruence. They see everything from a perspective of pragmatic idealism. They see what they think ought to be, but is not. The synthesizer is the youngest child of the Inbetweener, or the oldest child of the Challenger. The child of the Inbetweener is his pride and joy because, in his mind, he escaped to do something with his life by having this child. If it is the child of the Challenger then he, too, is proud because his child is following in his footsteps to conquer the world.

These are the children that are considered the third generation. Though they have a great life, it is this value system that begins to search for its roots. They or their children will cause the beginning of the search to understand where they come from and who their ancestors were. They develop greater selectivity and self-tolerance for who they are and desired to learn everything that has developed them the way they are.

Reader's Notes

ACTION STEPS

1. The first step of action to take is to begin by understanding who the church has been drawing.

2. The second step to take is to learn how many of these groups there are n the church.

3. The third step is to determine which of these groups are constant and which acts like a revolving door in the church.

4. The final step is to figure out where the church wants to concentrate resources and training to keep the church growing. That is, which of these groups will stay with the church to help it grow?

SUMMARY

This chapter is the mystery of why many Hispanic churches do not seem to want to grow. It has not been the leaders fault, nor bad administration, or Satan attacking the church. It is the changes in the community and what they have brought to the environment that have caused the church to seem impotent. Many good men and women have become frustrated to the point of quitting ministry because they just couldn't understand what was happening to them.

CHAPTER SIX
VISITOR ATTRACTION AND RETENTION
Profile of a Nation and a Church

In chapter four, I wrote of various cultures and subcultures and the need of churches to understand what has been happening to their communities. In chapter five, I argued that America has fast become a mission field and the need to understand the various generations which now exists in America. In this Chapter, I will discuss ways to attract and retain visitors by using some of the models that are currently being used by missionaries. If this nation has regressed into a mission status, then the church should treat it as a mission field and use mission-type strategies to evangelize.

Church leaders from England have been saying for a while that the church in America is fast becoming a post-Christian nation just like them. While that might be true to a certain point, it is also true that the United States does not have the same church foundation nor the same people groups as England does.

There are great differences between England and the united States. Differences in government structures have a tendency to help the church or hinder it. In England the government is more of an obstacle because there is no separation between governmental and the church.

In the United States there exists by law a separation of church and state. England has not had the influx of so many groups of people as have the United States. Just in these two distinctions alone, the results of the outcome of each nation in a similar situation can have grave differences. While England has regressed into a nation spiritually cold to evangelize, the United States, due to the influx of people searching for spiritual freedom, can continue the spark of revival in arrivals. Since its conception, the United States has been a parking lot for divers kinds of people fleeing their countries, because of religious or political persecution. Even today this wonderful country continues to open its arms to immigrants from around the globe. This influx of people coming from all over the world bring with them their customs and cultures. Combine that fact with the generations that have risen in these fast moving times, and this nation becomes one that is receiving and producing more unconnected people, more diverse in their own ways every year. No wonder this nation is a mission field.

Home grown cultures (the generations discussed in the last chapter) and immigrant cultures should be seen as a mission field which the church needs to penetrate. Churches have for the longest time been canvassing

Door to door searching for souls and reaping very little for their efforts. This strategy definitely needs to be reconsidered. Marvin K. Mayers in his book Christianity Confronts Culture gives a strategy for cross-cultural evangelism. He begins by explaining the development of the trust bond between the missionary and the people or culture he is trying to reach with the Gospel. He states in his book:

> "The trust bond is relatively easy to form when the participant's culture or subculture is similar. It is more difficult to form when such backgrounds are different... The greatest challenge in relationship occurs when the two parties disagree, and differences in culture and cultural perspective almost guarantee disagreement. The trust bond is a valuable tool in negating the adverse effects of disagreement." [1]

Trust must be established between the church, its leaders, congregation and the harvest field that the Holy Spirit wants cultivated. The profile of the entire church must be one that represents to the visitors being welcomed that the body of believers is reaching out to them in a genuine interest for the visitor's well being. Anything less is to present the body of Christ as not truly interested in the souls being saved for their sakes, but for the of the church and its needs.

---

[1] Marvin K Mayers, Confronts Culture Grand Rapids, MI: Zondervan Publishing House, 1987), pg. 6.

Mayers goes on to explain the importance of the question of trust:

> "The question of trust expressed as the prior question of trust, is a tool that can help one pause a moment before acting or responding. One can take a fresh look at interaction and allow sensitivity to come to the fore sensitivity to who the other is and what that one is feeling at that moment in time. The response made or action taken can be supportive and encouraging rather than degrading and destructive. The prior question of trust simply asks: is what I am doing, thinking, or saying, building trust or undermining trust? Is what I am doing, thinking, or saying potential for building trust or potential for undermining trust?" [2]

Building relationships between the visitors and the church is the greatest strategy to retain visitors continuously. The act of building relationships occurs when the church opens its doors to the public and the community. The more the church does this, the more visitors will be inclined to visit the church in an atmosphere of no commitment. The object of opening the doors of the church to the community is to seek those who have no relationships with anyone in the church. It is at this time that tho members of the church can begin to mix with the community and search for visitors with whom to converse. The

---

2 <u>Mayers</u>, pg. 7.

interest or a chance to minister to some problem idea behind conversing is to find a common ground of the visitor might have.

LEVELS OF TRUST

There are levels of trust in reaching out to visitors. For instance, consider a visitor who has just come to a church service. He is asked to sign the register and to give his address for future mailings. What if that visitor has had problems with people trying to sell him things or has had security problems? The visitor might be hesitant in giving his address so soon. Or, what if a visitor is coming to a social function and there encounters a pushy member who desires to give him a Bible study right there? Trust must be earned by being sensitive to what the visitor came for. As a visitor gives his permission to advance to the next level of trust, one should wait and pray to know how to better minister at that level. All trust begins at the level of friendship.

RECOGNITION OF TRUST TRANSFER

As the church begins to advance in its practice of building trust and confidence with people in the community, the people within that community will be open to advancement of the Gospel. This is what happened to Christ and the Samaritan woman at the well. Christ opened a conversation with the Samaritan man on the issue of natural water that led the woman to the need of spiritual water. By creating a bond of trust with her, she, in turn, went to her community and brought with her others with the same thirst for spiritual water. Christ was then invited to stay a while with them.

Likewise, the creation of trust between church people and visitors should be taken slowly. Cues will be given by the visitors when they are ready to advance to another level. Such cues can be permission to come to a party or special function of the visitor's home or other place. Another cue might be the need for a Bible study at home. It could come as a need in an emergency to the hospital, or calling for help when someone is ill and needs prayer.

Church members, too, can drop subtle cues for testing to see if the visitors are willing to remove their barriers of mistrust, One way is to invite the visitor to a greater commitment of time or energy. If the visitor agrees, then the relationship moves forward. If the visitor is hesitant, wait a while longer, but continue to monitor the visitor and pray. Either the visitor will desire to advance or will discontinue attending the church.

BONDING WITH OTHER CULTURES

Bonding with other cultures is one direct approach that a church can take to enter that culture. It is a good method to obtain maximum contact with the culture it is trying to reach. In order to obtain maximum contact with any culture, it is absolutely necessary to understand the identity of that society within the culture.

One local mission in an inner-city barrio hired their secretary from that neighborhood. The local mission needed someone who could read, write, and translate Spanish and English. The church placed flyers in the barrio, advertising a secretarial position. Ten women from that inner-city barrio arrived for the job interview. The church hired one of them, and that woman and her three children started coming to church. In a matter of months that woman had brought several families from her neighborhood.

The mission then repeated the same strategy and employed a gardener to keep the outside of the church clean. The mission placed the flyer in a bordering' neighborhood. The same thing happened. People that the gardener knew from his barrio started attend to the church.

The mission learned a valuable lesson of bonding with the surrounding communities. There are many ways of bonding; these are but a few examples. The main idea is that bonding must be done with the idea of building a relationship of trust, both from the group being reached, as well as the church reaching out.

CONTOURS OF THE CONGREGATION

The greatest challenge facing any church that desires to reach its community or generation is going to come from within. As stated earlier, man is his worst obstacle when it comes to doing God's will. Whether one is Mexican, Anglo, black, Asian, it matters not. The enemy sees no colors, only the people of God he wishes to destroy. The profile of the congregation is the most difficult to change, if change is needed. The pastor, his leaders, and the congregation will have to face this problem directly if the church truly wants to grow. The longer it takes for the church to realize that its community is changing and that it is not reaping visitors out of that culture, the harder it will be to make a smooth transition later.

There are two ways a congregation can face change. One way is to confront it, and the other is to run away from it. The congregation that confronts change will always find itself having to make adjustments in its daily life. The church that does not confront change remains settled in its old ways and considers only itself. The church feeds only itself and those who are like it, and it wants no one to challenge its ways. These are the churches at will probably die before they can be reborn. Church leaders need to realize what is happening around them and the changes occurring in their ministry area.

George Barna in his book **_The Frog in the Kettle_** has this to say about the condition of the church:

> "The Christian community in America might be expected to be more aware of current changes in the environment than the frog in the kettle. Yet, for the past two decades, at least, the church has been generally insensitive to those changes. We have continued to operate as though our environment has remained the same. Like the frog, we are faced with the very real possibility of dying because of our unresponsiveness to the changing world around us." [3]

If the insensitivity of church members and leader ers do not turn away the unchurched, the church's practices and method will. Though this book is directed to the

---

[3] George Barna <u>The Frog in the Kettle</u> (Ventura, CA: Regal Books, 1990), pg. 21-22.

Hispanic churches, most churches in America are facing similar problems. Churches, like nations, can become totally insensitive to the work of God.

Luis Palao, an evangelist in the southern Latino countries, spoke at Biola University where he said that he viewed the nation of Germany and its people like an old lady, postured like an old witch, with a little girl holding her hand. He went on to state that the old woman represented what the church had been before humanism, and the old witch represented what she was today. The little girl represented the young generations that were up and coming in a relationship with the old woman. The holding of hands explained their relationship. Truly, nations and countries that have been given much, such as Germany, England, France, Spain, and others, have had ample time to strengthen their Christianity. However, they did not, and they now find themselves trapped, and must, out of necessity, create new churches by equipping new missionaries to save the masses of people in their own countries.

Windows of opportunities do not remain open forever eventually they will close. It happened to Israel, once used mightily by God, and it can happen to the United

States off America. The question has been asked many times by church leaders, the media, and others: "Are we as Americans losing our grip on the Christianizing of our country?" If the answer is yes, how can it be turned around?

Material gradualism has taught the church to build bigger, better, prettier sanctuaries. It has led the church to labor hard in fund raising to pay for the brick wood sanctuaries, but has taught her nothing about the lost human temples. George Barna in his book **The Frog and the Kettle** explains just how much gradualism can destroy any institution:

> "The signs we need to perceive are not vague predictions about the future-many are present realities. The trouble is that they occur so gradually that we often do not notice them. It's like the familiar story of the frog and the kettle of water. Place a frog in boiling water and it will jump out immediately because it can tell that it's in a hostile environment. But place a frog in a kettle of room-temperature water and it will stay there, content with those surroundings. Slowly. Very slowly, increase the temperature of the water. This time, the frog doesn't leap out, but just stays there, unaware that the environment is changing. Continue to turn up tho burner until the water is boiling. Our Poor frog will be boiled, too–quite content, perhaps, but nevertheless dead."[4]

---

4 Barna, pg. 21.

The parents of the Boomers, the Silent generation, showed them by example to go to church, be faithful, and build up the material sanctuaries, and at the same time build their homes and families. The Boomer generation left the church and headed straight into the material world to get rich quickly and buy all the world has to offer. Both of these generations did little for the expansion of the work of God and the saving of souls. This is why the Buster generation is in its present condition. Their Christian values are all but gone along with what those in America have cherished the most-the family. Again, Barna puts it in perspective:

> "Consequently, America in the 90's is rotting from the inside out. We are suffering from constant, if almost imperceptible, shifts in perspective and behavior. As our population matures in technological sophistication and material comfort, we are losing our spiritual edge. We have embraced the means rather than the ends. Service to God has been replaced by a thirst for exaltation of self".[5]

This quote describes most the Boomer generation, but it also describes the spirit of the day. Look at the problems people are having in society. There is much with which to be concerned about the upcoming generations. Nothing that the Boomer or any other generation can come up

---

5 Barna, 23.

with can help them overcome the ills of their lives like the Word of God can.

The Bible is the only constant. The truth is ever present in this Book and has the answers for any problem anybody can have. God is immutable. It is only people and cultures that change. The problems that our society has may truly need different answers from those of the past, but the one Book that addresses the needs of today is the Word of God. Truth doesn't change, but how it is applied may. New solutions must be considered, but they must be immersed in the truth of God.

Again, Barna puts it into perspective when he writes:

> "What a tremendous opportunity the Christian community has to influence lives during this period! As Americans struggle to make sense of their new environment, the body of Christ has the chance to offer real, practical. Biblical solutions to our nation. However, the old approaches and traditional strategies for sharing our faith will no longer work in the 90's. We have to be clever enough to analyze our environment and provide creative responses to the challenges we face. Make no mistakes about it: the pressure on the Christian community is mounting. Typically, we have been five to ten years behind society, responding to changing conditions long after transitions have begun. And we have run out of time. If we want the Christian faith to remain a vibrant alternative to the world system, we must stop reacting and start anticipating" .6

---

5 Barna, pg. 23.

THE CHURCH AND TECHNOLOGY

The church certainly does have the answers the world needs because the Word of God can still be effective in human lives. The church must be aligned with the truth and be living by its standards. The church today has the technology at its fingertips to help it. Christian men and women work in companies using technology and information systems like never before in the history of the church. All the church needs to learn are new ways of sharing it with the unchurched. It is crucial in today's world to be up to date in utilizing information systems, because the tools used by the church of yesteryear will not convince the unchurched that Christianity is still pertinent to the needs of the 21st century people.

If the church is not able to attract the lost, they will keep on looking until they are ensnared by America's cults. Since many of these unchurched people view the church as irrelevant, they will find other religions such as Mormonism, Islam, Buddhism, and various New Age cults who are more attractive.

READER'S NOTES

PEOPLE'S PATHWAYS AND FLOW

The business market has for years been following people's pathways and the flow of money coming from these pathways. That is to say, the business market has studies showing where people go and what they buy. The market then takes the information, creates stores where people congregate, and sell what the people most likely need.

K-mart is not going to build a new store in a location of which they have no knowledge. The financial risk is too high. They would rather spend money in research that will tell them
what kind of people live in which communities, if their market will meet their needs, and if the people in that community are ling to pay for it.

The church has to use similar techniques to assess various communities to attract the unchurched. Should they use inhouse programs such as a fully planned Sunday schools, children programs, Christian schools, day care facilities, formal or informal worship services, and other community-based programs? In other words, will Mohammed (the visitors) come to the mountain (the church) or will the mountain come to Mohammed?

Many churches become frustrated because they spend much of their time, resources and money on in house programs to capture the people the congregation has invited, but the number of people that they are able to bring in is very little. It is obvious that many congregations have too little of a pool of unchurched friends. The fact of the matter is that the church often spends a lot and gets very little in return.

By understanding people's pathways and flow, the church is able to know where people will be trafficking and the rate of that traffic. This is valuable information to any group of people trying to get a handle on visitor attraction and retention.

The Holy Spirit is the agent on earth to guide the church in the search for the lost. In Acts 1:8, Luke gives one of the last' commandments of Jesus when he writes:

> "But ye shall receive power, after that the Holy Ghost is come upon you: and ye shall be witnesses unto me both in Jerusalem, and in Judea, and in Samaria, and unto the uttermost part of the earth." 7

Dr. Luke goes on to state the fact that it is the Holy Spirit Who adds daily to the church in chapter 2: 46-47:

> "And they, continuing daily with one accord in the temple, and breaking bread from house to house, did eat their meat with gladness and singleness of heart, praising God, and having favour with all the people.

---

7 Acts 1:8, Jesus commands His disciples to go to Jerusalem, Judea, Samaria, and the whole earth.

> And the Lord added to the . church daily such as should be saved."8

It is the Holy Spirit who guides the church or the believers in seeking that which is lost in the community. The Holy Spirit resides in the believers because of this, the Gospel becomes a caring tool in the believer. Where the believer is there also is the Holy Spirit. He is trying to match the area in which He has been laboring with believers to deliver the living Word.

This concept is very true because the Spirit of Christ is already at work reaching and calling people. The Gospel of Luke has a similar idea in chapter 10. Christ is sending out the seventy disciples to go into villages and cities. When they enter into a home they are told to heal the sick and to proclaim that the kingdom' of God has come nigh unto them. He writes:

> *"After these things the Lord appointed other seventy also, and sent them two and two before his face into every city and place, whither he himself would come. Therefore said he unto them, The harvest truly is great, but the laborers are few: pray ye therefore the Lord of the Harvest, that he would send forth laborers into his harvest ... And into whatsoever houso ye enter, first say, Peace be to this house. And if the son of peace be there, your peace shall rest upon it: if not, it shall turn to you again ... And heal the sick that are therein, and say unto them,*

---

8 **Acts 2:46,47, Luke's conversation as to what transpired in those days.**

The kingdom of God is come nigh unto you."9

Matthew also gives a glimpse of what Christ commanded His disciples at the mountain when he writes:

> "Then the eleven disciples went away into Galilee, into a mountain where Jesus had appointed them. And when they saw him, they worshipped him: but some doubted. And Jesus came and spake unto them, saying, All power is given unto me in heaven and in earth. Go ye therefore, and teach all nations, baptizing them in the name of the Father, and of the Son, and of the Holy Ghost:"10

If the church is having trouble attracting visitors to the church building, then take the church to where the Spirit of Christ is ministering. This seems to be where the problem is most prevalent. The church was never told to wait for the souls to wake up from their sleep and come to a church building. Church members are are to go wherever the Holy Spirit is ministering and join in on the harvesting. Believers are to set up places of worship whether they be in tents or under trees, and there preach the Gospel. This thinking may sound foreign to some, but this seems to be implied in the reading of the Scriptures. The church, that is body of Christ, is failing to

---

9 Luke 10:1-9, Luke's description as to what the seventy should do

10 Matthew 28:16-19, Matthew's version as to Jesus' command to witness.

understand the mandates and the processes it takes to bring the Gospel to the lost, and not bring lost to the church. Finding the lost and pricking their life and hearts is the job of the Holy Spirit. The job of the church is to take the good news of Jesus Christ as true born again children have been redeemed with the power of the blood of Christ and share with the lost the miracles that have happened. The testimonies will give the lost proof that what is claimed is truth. Luke, in the book of the Acts, confirms this:

> "Then Philip went down to the city of Samaria, and preached Christ unto them. And the people with one accord gave heed unto those things which Philip spake, hearing and seeing the miracles which he did ... And there was great joy in that city ... But when they believed Philip preaching the things concerning the kingdom of God, and the name of Jesus Christ, they were baptized, both men and women.[11]

This is why the tent meetings and healing crusades attract so many people. The evangelist seeks the guidance of the Spirit of God to know where to take his tent and have a revival to reach the people who need Christ. The people of God too often stay in church buildings, beating the drums of Christ and His salvation to communities that are deaf to drums.

---

[11] Acts 8:5-11, Christ's exhortation to His disciples about loving one another.

God's people must find the pathways of people in need and there seek ways to present the Gospel effectively. This is the front line of the war. At this juncture in this study, all that can be presented are the principles of getting to the front line. The details of fighting the war are too numerous and different in every battle.

What are some of the pathways that should be considered? Depending on the generation, culture, or subculture in the ministry area of the church, the church should be thinking about shopping malls, neighborhoods, city or community parks, and recreational and sports facilities. Other "hangout" areas such as laundromats, supermarkets, convalescent and general hospitals, It even funeral services, can present opportunities to share the Gospel. Almost any place that creates people pathways and flow can be considered as the frontline of evangelism.

The challenge of the church leadership is going to be to educate its members in finding creative ways of presenting the gospel without causing resistance, rejection or trouble in the public sector. The following scenario is an sample that has been tried and found most useful and successful. The church basketball team asks their friends or invites those people at the public basketball courts to join in on the game. All that should be sought an activity such as this is mutual friendship and the desire to play as many games as possible.

G.Is, Silents, and Boomers love a good challenge. We need to address the unchurched on areas of pride, joy, pleasure, and the like for topics of exercises Evangelism. The conversation of the Christian team should be a simple strategy of getting the most information about the unchurched opponents as possible. If the church teams wins, take the losers of the game out to lunch.

Continue to work on the team concept of both the church side and the unchurched side. Solidify a relationship between the two sides. Once in a while change partners as to break the "side" mentality. Continue to work on the conversation and the spirit of the game. Work on the trust levels and the bond relationship.

If there is court near the church, have a couple of games there. If there is a court on the church grounds, have a match when the church has an outside activity, and have them stay for it. Remember, the object is not to immediately get them to repent and be baptized, but to create a friendship. The basketball activity should not go on forever; its ultimate aim should always be to reach them with the gospel.

SUMMARY

There are at least two attraction phases in the process of attracting visitors to a church. The initial attraction phase begins and ends in the field with the evangelist. A new attraction phase begins in the sanctuary life with many of the members of the church. The first attraction phase needs as many people as possible. The second attraction phase starts with an usher and continues to add until the visitor has contacted most of the members of the church.

The retention phase begins late in the initial attraction base and continues into the sanctuary life phase. In the retention phase, individuals initially can be helpers of the evangelist in the field, so that the visitor can begin forming trust with them also. They should act as helpers to the team members so as not to disrupt the evangelist's relationship with the visitor. When the visitor is ready to come to church, the initial retention phase individuals will be part of the committee members that will help the visitor transition to the congregation. Because the retention phase individuals have already formed a trust with the visitor, he will be more apt to not feel lonely, insecure, or frightened by all that is happening around him. The visitor will be guided and counseled with everything that is that is happening to him by the committee members. Meanwhile, the evangelists should stay in the field and continue searching for more souls.

What was gained in the field can be lost in the sanctuary, if caution is not taken to protect the transition of the newcomer. The principles that the soldiers have at the front line must also be part of the church's total philosophy, exemplified by all members of the church. If this is not achieved, the visitors will not identify with the church's profile and identity. The visitors will find themselves confused and misled. The retention phase will cease at this point, and the visitors will not come again. They may come into contact again with the evangelist and explain why they do not want to return to church, or they will simply disappear. Visitors who do not come back a second time to church probably noticed a big difference between the evangelist and the members of the church, scaring them into not going there again.

This scene is where local churches tend to lose visitors, brought in by hard working members in the field. The field personnel have labored to adapt to the needs of the unchurched and have, as much as they can, presented an image that will win the visitor's trust to commit to at least a visit. When the visitors is then taken to the sanctuary, the visitor may experience a culture shock. His expectations of the church were based on the profile evangelist and not on the real contour of the church. The visitor is then discouraged in what he expected, wanted, or needed.

Reader's Notes

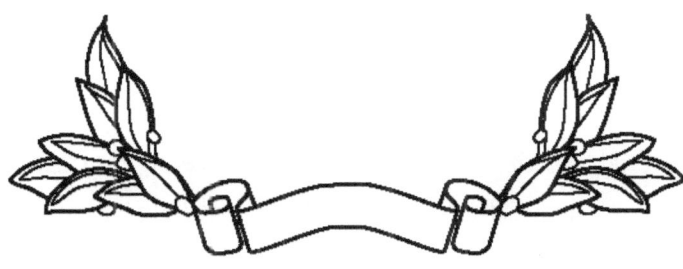

CHAPTER SEVEN
CONCLUSION TO THE BOOK

I have been working with a pastor by the name of Jim Mena, who happens to be my wife's cousin, and is currently tho pastor of a church in Redlands, California. He was telling me that he had discovered a fishing hole that he thought would help him a lot. I responded and told him, "Jim since when have you taken up fishing?" He responded that the fishing hole was called in Spanish, "El ministerio de la lunderia," the laundromat ministry. He went on to tell me that near his church there was a laundromat that many people use. While they did their wash, they had to literally spend wasted time because there was nothing else to do. He was going to get some of his people to park close to the laundromat and share their faith and testimonies with the "laundromatians".

Another pastor in Macallen, Texas, by the name of Arcadio Pena discovered a different sort of a well ministry. Some members of his congregation do business in the Swap Meets and they saw an opportunity to minister to a lot of people there. So the church regularly rents a booth at this open air swap meets and place Christian music and pass out tracts.

The church needs to explore and discover new methods finding, locating and creating avenues of contact with the unchurched. There are many open air activities, like: Rodeos, main street events, cook outs, parades, car-shows, and many other of types of events.

Linking the Unchurched to the Congregation

Linking the unchurched to the church or a congregation is a necessary step in any evangelist's mind. Once a water hole has been established, a number of the congregation should go and take water. The more people from the church meet people at the water hole, the more contacts church members will established with the churched.

Consider again the laundromat scenario. How can this water hole be linked with Pastor Jim Mena's congregation? One sure way is to expose as many of the members of the church in Redlands to this water hole to come and meet those who patron there. They could possibly even come and wash clothes there.

Another way is to ask for permission from the owners of the laundromat to hang a bulletin board somewhere on a wall in the laundromat.. This bulletin board can act like a sign to point people to the church in Redlands. One way is to place small holding racks at the base of the bulletin board to place tracts and any information the church wants to share with the people that go there. Another way is to announce special activities that are going to be held at the sanctuary, a park or someone's house.

Another way is to share information of upcoming special speakers, or offer classes on ESL-(English as a second language), A note could be posted that offered to have someone from the church come and do tax returns on the church premises.

Another note the church can post is directions to the church, along with a picture of the pastor and his family on the bulletin board. A picture of the sanctuary and of some of the people that have come and joined the church from that place is another option.

The church should be aware if what the church is offering is what these people like or need. If the people take the literature and the church gets them to come, then it is obvious that the material is being used. Write on the material to bring the note to a function to collect a prize is another indication that it is working if they attend the function. Remember also the literature has to be in their language.

What Well Ministries Have in Common

1. People must come to them sooner or later.
2. When they do come, most of their time is spent free. The actual work takes only a few minutes.
3. They do not bring anything to occupy them since they are not going to be there very long.

4. The setting of well ministries are usually lonely and isclated.

BIBLICAL WELL MEETINGS

1. Christ at the well with the Samaritan woman
2. Abraham s servant in search of Issac's wife
3. The well from which Moses drank after leaving Egypt and crossing the desert

There are other biblical examples of wells, but the fact of the matter is to learn how to find and use ministries like these for evangelistic work. There are many such water holes to work evangelistically, this is the reason to do an assessment of the community which the church desires to target. The more one knows about a place, the more that can be done to use it for evangelistic purposes. Use all the information that has been given in this book to help understand better the people being targeted. Oh yes, and remember, that generations do make a difference.

READER'S NOTES

EVALUATION OF THE BOOK
THE INCEPTION OF THE PROJECT

It has now been twenty-four years since the desire began to write this project. It did not start right off as a book concept. The desire started more like a need to understand how to reach, Hispanics with the Word of God. It then grew with many questions that had no real answers. It moved from questions, to frustrations, to prayers, and back to questions, always being left with a feeling of inadequacy. After searching God in prayer for answers, He has led to this work. It is to Him that all the honor and all the glory is given for what He has taught this writer through so many men and women.

When given the green light to search for a topic for this dissertation, the work began to find the right material to contemplate writing this book. No one outside of this writer's wife and God knew the burden to learn and process what God's church needs. In a way, studying the last fifteen years in school have been easy, being that the Holy Spirit has been the agent in this conclusion. On the other hand, whenever a person has been driven, the challenge to find answers to questions that few have even begun to contemplate, is a very difficult situation.

RESEARCH AND DEVELOPMENT

The research part of this dissertation has taken longer than what was first imagined. The time involved in the field alone has been six years. Those years have been the accumulation of records, data, charts, and pertinent information. Questionnaires were formulated as best as possible to ascertain data that otherwise would not have been available. This writer had the privilege of working with many pastors in the field in acquiring information that probably had not been gathered before. Altogether the research used directly and indirectly with pastors was about 300 churches, missions. The work spent in the field has led to a well-spent time in gathering information and trying various new things with pastors. Many of these pastors were able to grow the church they pastored, because of these studies, activities and programs.

The development of this material in this dissertation was designed in the field to be used in the field. Various churches needed the material from the chapters in this manuscript. For example, many Hispanic pastors knew about the influx of Hispanics into their churches and had tackled the diversity of the problems that came with that influx. The problems proved to be too complex for them. The pastors had little success in integrating the various groups. They had success with maybe one or even two groups that were very similar, but all in all they were not able to keep all that God had given them.

Chapter one was designed to help in this matter. Chapter one talked about the history of the Hispanic culture, and the development of the Hispanic church.

Another problem encountered in the field while doing research and then trying to develop this project was the lack of pastors knowing how to develop or design leadership vision in a their respective churches. Again, this was the reason for designing chapter two.

Chapter two deals with the strengths and weaknesses of the local church. This chapter attempted to show where the local church was in relation to its resources: manpower, training, morale, facilities, etc. Before an aggressive adventure in attracting souls can take place, the membership of the local church must take into account all that is at its disposal. Christ said in the Gospel of Matthew not to undertake building a tower before knowing what it will take to see it through to completion. Many pastors had not learned how to read changing communities, thus their churches had undergone enormous pressures and financial losses because of it.

Chapter three enables leaders to assess community needs. In this chapter, pastors read and understand about communities and cultures that are going through changes.

While pondering the many needs of the churches in the field, a pattern to the reason why many churches were unsuccessful, for the most part, in attracting or retaining visitors began to emerge. The pattern developed is what many innovative pastors have learned. For the most part, pastors play the part of the man inside a large forest who all he can see are trees. If there are no directions or signs, or if he does not know the ways out of that forest, he is basically lost.

The forest ranger will study a forest first and note the various signs and special effects of said forest before going in. So it is with many pastors. They get right into pastoring and build themselves a church without any regard to vision, direction, or the kind of people that their church will be drawing from the community. This is the reason why chapter four needed to be included. It discusses what generational ideology is all about and what impact this concept can have upon cultures and on the church. Current generations in America were individually described and addressed as means to evangelize.

New methodology in reaching Hispanic visitors is given 'in chapter five. Organizational churches tend to be too busy in their day to day business of running the church that they are unable to figure out a good methodology for evangelism. The profile of the church and that of the evangelist is the focus of this methodology.

In research for this book manuscript, only two quality books on visitor attraction were discovered. One was very old, and the other quite recent. Both set the agenda and background for dealing with visitors from a perspective of an in-house program. Further research led to the concept as to why churches were having a difficult time attracting the lost. The evaluation of churches, their values, methods, programs, and activities they used, to attract souls, revealed that they were searching for people that looked for and wanted the same things the church did. Field research into their communities began to profile the people living around the church ministry area. To this writer's surprise, most of the people of the community did not match the profile of the church. The people of the community were not the kind of visitors the church wished to attract.

The profile of the community and that of the church did not match in identity and self-image. Either the church was too unresponsive for the community's spiritual need, or the community was too indifferent for the church. This mismatch of profiles was alarming. No wonder the church is having so much trouble reaching the people in its community.

In most cases when there is quite a lot of indifference between church and community, it is because the community has undergone a change, and the church has cut itself off from the recipients that it needed to continue its growth. The result was a church that had continued to develop in a community that no longer offered the church the kind of numbers it needed to grow. Any church that finds itself in this predicament must consider a methodology of reaching whoever resides in the community.

This has led to the development of the chapters in such an order that the pastors, leaders, or evangelists could know what they are up against in order to begin a strategy in reaching the unchurched.

The programs that need to be constructed to best have an impact in the need community will have to be community based ministries. The church will launched these ministries based on the research the church does. These community based ministries must function on community property and not the church's property. These programs or ministries will have to be very close to the people they are trying to reach. As people are visited and relationships established, the people in these programs will undoubtedly generate homes from where they can minister. The cell ministry or house church programs can take effect then. The Christian workers will he able to try all kinds of new and innovative programs that can minister to the whole family being reached right in their own homes. As trust and bonding occurs, they can decide whether a new church or mission ought to be started, or taken to the sanctuary for further bonding with the mother church.

THE READERS

The readers for this dissertation were chosen from three areas namely: theological and Scriptural background of whom Dr. Wayne Flory, professor of Biblical Studies department of the University of Biola in the city of La Mirada, California, was so kind to review. Dr. Wayne Flory addressed several areas and was very helpful in aiding me to think through the use of the spiritual gifts section. He also suggested including with this dissertation some of the evaluating instruments resources. He thought that it would be helpful for the reader to have those in the dissertation to refer to them. A long time friend and pastor Benjamin Quiroz also read and critiqued it from a pastor's point of view.

Laura Mcintosh is my dissertation proof reader who critiqued the grammatical and writing style and structure. Laura had this to say about this work. *"The strong point of this paper is in the style. The vocabulary is clear and concise, making the paper understandable and easy to read for the average reader."* She went on to state that *"each point of the paper was explained thoroughly before attempting to discuss another aspect."* She stated that the organization, transitions, and over all flow of the paper gave it good reading style. She also pointed to some weaknesses in writing which this writer has suffered for some time. She stated that the paper needed to be written more objectively. The usage of the first person should be avoided. She also pointed out that the writer needed to place more attention to consistency in some areas of format and grammar.

Pastor Quiroz found the dissertation very enlightening. He liked most all of the material, and said that it was about time a book like this be written for Hispanic pastors. While he gave great reviews on the book, he did point out one large weakness. That weakness was that there was very little material given in the areas of how to's in visitor attraction and retention. This writer is very aware of this weakness, and hopes to do something about it soon.

He also suggested that each chapter be somehow integrated with the title.

EVALUATIONS AND CONCLUSIONS

As stated previously, a great attempt has been labored to try to educate the average Hispanic pastor in the areas that have caused a lack of visitor attraction and retention. The manuscript is in dire need of more examples in all of the chapters as to how to connect the chapter material to the growing understanding of visitor attraction and retention.

QUESTIONS FOR FURTHER STUDY

It is obvious now that more thinking is necessary to answer the question of how to attract and retain the visitors. The following questions may be of use for further study.

1. Is servant leadership a style that can be effective in the Hispanic church and congregation?
2. Can church officers work together to develop that style in their mutual ministries?
3. Every pastor has different gifts. No pastor can be equally skillful in all the areas described in this chap ter. How can a church staff and leadership share in the tasks of ministry so as to free the pastor to make use of his great skills?

4. What opportunities does a congregation give the Hispanic pastor for spiritual renewal and continuing education?
5. What opportunities for church officer training does the pastor and congregation provide?

IMPLICATIONS FOR CHURCH AT LARGE

The implications of this manuscript may well fit most of the other ethnic churches. It is probably true that many of the facets of this work could very well be adapted to the Korean churches, since that group of people have many similarities with Hispanic churches.

The church at large will probably be most interested in any of the chapters, especially in those that delineate the Hispanic people more. This is because many English churches are now starting to work with other minorities.

SUMMARY

The writer has certainly learned much through the writing of this manuscript. It is hoped that it will honor God. It is this writer's sincere wish and prayer that it may be of benefit to the Hispanic pastors when this project is finally finished. Much thanks and appreciation is given to all those who have helped in the process of writing and editing this work.

Reader's Notes

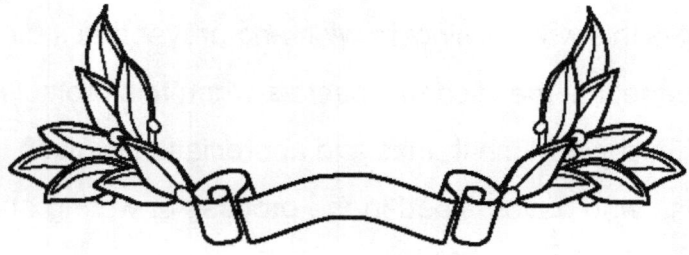

BIBLIOGRAPHY

Aldrich, Joe. Life Style Evangelism. Portland, OR.: Multnomah Press, 1981.

Am, Win. The Church Growth Ratio. Pasadena, CA.: Church Growth, Inc., 1987.

Barna, George. The Frog in the Kettle. Ventura, CA.: Regal Books, 1990.

Damazio, Frank. The Making of a Leader. Portland OR.: Bible Temple Publishing, 1988.

Ellicott, Charles John. Ellicot's Bible Commentary. Grand Rapids, MI.: Zondervan Publishing House, 1971.

Engstrom, Ted W. The Making of a Christian Leader. Grand Rapids, MI.: Pyrenees Books, House, 1976.

Gazoqsky, Richard. Just Add Water. San Francisco, CA.: Voice of Pentecost, Inc, 1992.

Hadaway, Kirk C. Church Growth Principles: Separating Fact from Fiction, Nashville, TN.: Broadman Press, 1991.

Marvis, Curry W. Advancing the Smaller Church. Grand Rapids, MI: Baker, 1957.

Mayers, Marvin K. Christianity Confronts Culture. Grand Rapids, Mi.: Zondervan Publishing House,1989.

McKenna, David L. Power to Follow, Grace to Lead. Dallas, TX.: Word Publishing House, 1989,

Miller, John C. <u>Outgrowing the ingrown Church</u> Grand Rapids, MI.: Zondervan Publishing. 1986.

Moberg, David o. <u>The church or Social Institution</u>. Englewood Cliffs, NJ.: Prentice Hall, Inc., 1962.

Reeves, Daniel. <u>Always Advancing: Modern Strategies for Church Growth.</u> San Bernardino, CA.: Here's Life Publishers, Inc., 1984.

Strauss, William and Neil Howe. <u>Generations: The History of America's Future</u>. New York, NY.: William Morrow & Company, Inc., 1991.

Tillapaugh, Frank R. <u>Unleashing the Church</u>. Ventura, CA.: Regal BOOKS, 1982.

Tillapaugh, Frank R. <u>Unleashing Your Potential</u>. Ventura, CA.: Regal Books, 1988.

Towns, Elmer L. <u>America's Fastest Growing Churches.</u> Nashville, TN.: Impact Books, 1972.

www.ingramcontent.com/pod-product-compliance
Lightning Source LLC
Chambersburg PA
CBHW022005160426
43197CB00007B/283